MEDICAL MURDER

DISTURBING CASES OF DOCTORS WHO KILL

DR ROBERT M. KAPLAN

MEDICAL MURDER
This edition published in 2010 by Summersdale Publishers Ltd.

First published by Allen & Unwin Ltd in 2009

Summersdale Publishers Ltd
46 West Street
Chichester
West Sussex
PO19 1RP
UK

www.summersdale.com

Printed and bound in Great Britain

ISBN: 978-1-84953-036-1

Contents

About the author

Dr Robert M. Kaplan leads a double life. In his day job he is a forensic psychiatrist, Clinical Associate Professor at the Graduate School of Medicine, University of Wollongong, and associate member of the South African Association of Professional Archaeologists. In his other life, he is a writer, historian and student of the vagaries of human nature. He has written and published on medicine, psychiatry, history and crime; subjects include Dr Radovan Karadzic, Adolf Hitler, James Joyce and Sigmund Freud. His interests include serial killers and medical crime; the origin of modern humans; Jewish life and Talmudic thinking; medical messiahs, moral panic and modern witchhunts.

He has broadcast on ABC Radio, given talks to a range of audiences and published in *Australasian Psychiatry*, the *British Medical Journal*, *South African Medical Journal*, *Medical Observer* and *Scope*. He was consultant to Professor Charles van Onselen for his book *The Fox and the Flies: The World of Joseph Silver, Racketeer and Psychopath*. He regularly goes to South Africa to visit museums, prehistoric diggings and encounter some of the best historians and archaeologists in the world.

Born in Edinburgh, raised in South Africa and living in Australia for several decades, he is waiting for the authorities to deport him. To the small circle of private individuals prepared to admit that they know him, he is regarded as a more than fair cook, a feckless word spinner and obsessive alliterator who keeps unreliable hours and is utterly unable to take anything seriously. He maintains an unfulfilled ambition to complete his autobiography, working title *Memoirs of a Marginal Medical Student*.

Prologue

In January 2000, world-wide headlines announced that English general practitioner Dr Harold Shipman was found guilty of murdering fifteen of his patients. Before his trial, many had assumed that Shipman was an overzealous doctor doing no more than 'easing the passing' of dying patients. But the evidence showed otherwise; Shipman deliberately murdered not just fifteen, but several hundred patients in the most efficient mechanical and indifferent fashion, making him a hitherto unparalleled medical serial killer.

Shipman's American epigone, aspiring neurosurgeon Dr Michael Swango, spread his net across the US, Zimbabwe and Zambia, leaving a trail of bodies in his wake. Sydney psychiatrist Dr Harry Bailey killed close to a hundred patients with Deep Sleep Therapy, a discredited and dangerous form of treatment. Dr Radovan Karadzic, the psychiatrist who led the Bosnian Genocide, shelled the hospital in Sarajevo where he had worked, killing colleagues and patients.

The phenomenon of medical killing has been largely ignored and there has been no attempt to understand the basis for such extreme behaviour. In this book, I explore *clinicide*—a new term—defined as the death of multiple patients in the course of treatment by a doctor. The study of clinicide raises powerful and disturbing questions: why do doctors deliberately kill their patients, ignore appalling death rates, or use their medical skills to participate in horrendous experiments, torture or genocidal murder in the service of the state?

Medical murders are appalling but unusual crimes. It is a paradox, considering the extraordinary effort, discipline and devotion that it takes to become a doctor when throughout history medicine has been regarded as a sacred calling. While the incidence of medical killing is very low, this is little consolation to the victims or their families.

I have examined clinicide in the context of the history of medicine, forensic psychiatry and sociology. The role of the healer, medicine man or doctor is universal and little, aside from advances in technology, will change this. The motives of doctors are as much an expression of the prevailing culture as scientific progress which, in many cases is suborned by its practitioners for all too-human motives.

I explore medical killers over time, focusing on Harold Shipman, Michael Swango, Harry Bailey, John Bodkin Adams and Radovan Karadzic.

That some doctors become killers says much about human nature, society and the practice of medicine. But it should be remembered that very, very few members of a great profession follow this path. The practice of medicine is an inherently good activity, and it is to the credit of the profession that there are so few killers. I hope this book will make a contribution to keeping it this way.

Dr Robert M. Kaplan
March, 2009

1

The rise and fall of the medical calling

The most incisive words on medical murder were written in 1978 by forensic pathologist Keith Simpson:

> Doctors are in a particularly good position to commit murder and escape detection. Their patients, sometimes their own fading wives, more often merely aging nuisances, are in their sole hands. 'Dangerous drugs' and powerful poisons lie in their professional bags or in their surgery. No one is watching or questioning them, and a change in symptoms, a sudden grave 'turn for the worst' or even death is for them alone to interpret.

Doctors, Simpson pointed out, authorise the removal of a dead patient by writing the death certificate. If they take the law into their own hands, it is only likely to emerge through chance, whisperings or rumour, or careless disposal of the body. That medical murder emerges so seldom, considering the number of practitioners, is either a testimony to their moral fibre or the ease with which they can conceal crime.

English psychiatrist Herbert Kinnell rates doctors as the greatest killers among all the professions. Doctors as a group are murderous: they kill family and friends; they kill their patients; and they kill strangers, chiefly for political reasons, by torture, mass murder or genocide.

Medicine has always had an attraction to those interested in power over life and death, status and the acquisition of wealth. The first factor in its appeal to potential killers was the institutionalisation of medicine. Legitimisation put the medical profession in a position of power, authority and status it has ever since been reluctant to cede, a built-in factor attracting a certain kind of psychopath.

As the nature of medical practice changed, the number of doctors being trained expanded in tandem with the population. Welcome as this development was—because it meant the medical population was more representative of the community—it increased the possibility of someone who was a completely unknown quantity graduating and going into practice. Before, say, World War II, a psychopathic individual intrigued by exploiting the power over life and death in this setting would have had to choose a low-status alternative career, or even fake their credentials. After institutionalisation there was no need for these machinations; with a little effort, medical schools became an open market. Dr Marcel Petiot, for example, who worked in the early part of the twentieth century, only had eight months' training when he came out of military service. Linda Hazzard, who killed numerous people with starvation diets in the United States and New Zealand, had a dubious osteopathic qualification and was allowed to call herself a doctor by virtue of a grandfather clause in one of the states where she worked.

In a setting where medical practice is defensive and insecure, to say the least, there are any number of opportunities for the psychopathic doctor. And the reckless treatment killer, driven by mania, narcissism or hubris, can find any number of cracks in which to insert themselves in the medical edifice.

Clinicide means the death of numerous patients during treatment by a doctor. Like any crime, clinicide is a complex behaviour affected by social, cultural, psychological and forensic factors. Just as the classification of illness and the practice of doctors reflect the society in which they occur, so do the circumstances of clinicide.

Clinicide can be divided into several categories:

Medical serial killing

The image of a 'serial killer' is not a medical doctor in a white jacket. But when doctors turn on patients because they derive some perverse pleasure from the act of killing, they tend to be prolific murderers. While reckless, incompetent, inept, mad or just plain dangerous doctors have been around for as long as medicine has been practised, medical serial killing is a relatively new phenomenon. Serial killers are obviously not mentally balanced individuals. Nonetheless, there is a certain inner rationality to their actions—they know that they are engaged in murder, and they go to great lengths to plan out the continued fulfilment of their murderous fantasies.

French doctor Marcel Petiot left a trail of bodies wherever he practised. His period of destruction probably extends from 1926 (if not before) until 1944, and an estimate of 100–200 victims is reasonable, making him the worst serial killer in French history. Dr Harold Shipman, easily the worst serial killer in the United Kingdom, was killing patients from the time he went into practice in 1974, continuing with only a year's break when he was receiving treatment for drug addiction, until his arrest in 1998. Dr Michael Swango killed 60 patients from the time of his internship in 1983 until he left Zambia in 1996 (with several years away when he was in jail and out of practice). Between them, Shipman and Swango are credited with at least 313 deaths. The worst Scandinavian serial killer is Dr Arnfinn Nesset,[1] credited with 137 murders within half a decade. These figures are far in excess of what the average serial killer attains, and reveals just how dangerous a medical serial killer can be when unleashed.

Treatment killing

Treatment killing refers to multiple patient deaths in which it is not immediately obvious that the doctor intended the patients to die. A separate category is merited because the question of intentionality (motivation) and self-awareness of the harmful nature of the action is blurred in these cases. Treatment killers are either doctors who are mentally impaired, or those who do not have a mental illness as such but view their patients as mere accessories to their own grandiose role, no more than objects who ought to be grateful for any treatment they receive, regardless of the outcome.

Doctors with serious mental illness are a problem as old as medicine. When a prominent physician or surgeon is involved, it is described as an example of the 'Great Man syndrome'. These doctors have such authority and charisma that underlings are always reluctant to challenge them to stand down—and they are even less likely to obey when told.

Treatment killer doctors only achieve recognition, and most reluctantly so, when the extent of the deaths associated with their treatment becomes exposed to the public. There is shock, horror and outrage, often leading to disciplinary inquiries or manslaughter charges. To the onlooker, investigator or general public, this is predicated on the idea that incompetence, wilful or witless, caused the patient deaths, and they were not deliberate or intended. As the courts put it, there is no apparent motive.

Such doctors develop a God complex, getting a vicarious thrill out of ending suffering and determining when a person dies. Peter Smerick, former FBI criminal profiler, describes two types of treatment killers:

1. The *Hero Killer* doctor would put a patient under great risk. If they save the patient, they are a hero. If the patient dies, the killer will say 'So what?'

2. The *Mercy Killer* doctor will rationalise that they are concerned about the suffering of their patients and put them out of their misery. They count on the fact that autopsies are usually not performed when a terminally ill patient dies.

Doctors, particularly specialists, are not only trained but expected to provide optimum care at all times, to seek help or second opinions regardless of vanity or fear of criticism. Their role is to take responsibility for the patient's care as far as can be reasonably expected. When the death list progresses beyond two, or four or twenty patients, it is not possible for a doctor to continue treating patients without some awareness that they may cause death. At some level, these doctors realise what they are doing, but this is countered by an overweening refusal to acknowledge the reality or desist. Denial alone can't explain why a surgeon or psychiatrist can ignore death after death after death of patients under their care. The cases of Dr Ferdinand Sauerbruch, Dr Hamilton Bailey and Dr Harry Bailey show how treatment killers operate.

Mass murderers

Mass or political murderers fall into another category. Their activities are so extreme and appalling that attempts to portray them as serial killers operating on a wider front are misleading. Doctors have frequently been accomplices in state-led repression, brutality and genocide, in direct contravention to their sanctioned role to relieve suffering and save lives. Doctors have performed inhumane experiments on victims, participated in torture and directed programs to exterminate the enemy. In addition, they have beaten, tortured and killed victims for no other reason than they had the power to do it at the time, and gave every indication of enjoying what they did. In doing so, they became mass murderers on an exponential scale, making any comparison with a doctor killing his own patients untenable.

In the last decade, there have been any number of reports of doctors participating in state abuse of human rights, usually in their treatment of detained enemy suspects. The most recent example of this is Dr Radovan Karadzic, a practising psychiatrist who led the Bosnian Genocide. Forces under Karadzic's direct command were responsible for mass atrocities, leading to 250,000 deaths and up to one million homeless. What's more, Karadzic's motivation was not purely political as he used his psychological training to direct terror tactics.

While these three categories of clinicide differ greatly, they all share one element: although society places an enormous amount of trust in doctors to prevent harm and promote health, these perpetrators violate that trust in the most shocking and horrific manner.

> A physician is obligated to consider more than a diseased organ, more even than the whole man—he must view the man in his world.
>
> Harvey Cushing

In order to understand clinicide, it is important to understand the terrain in which doctors operate: the medical profession, its history and culture. Seeking treatment for an illness or injury is a specifically human activity. It requires a sense of being unwell, and desiring to alter this. Dr William Osler, the most famous physician of his time, went so far as to state that 'The desire to take medicine is perhaps the greatest feature which distinguishes man from animals'. This produced *homo therapeuticus*, the medicine-taking animal: you and me.

While this pill-popping perspective may reflect the particularly skewed vision of a physician, Osler had a point. Medicine, in the form of healing, has been with us for as long as we have been sentient human beings. Rock painting and engraving, which goes back 30,000 years, arose from shamanic trance states during healing dances. The shamans communicated with spirits for the purposes of healing illness, breaking drought periods, finding animal herds and promoting group cohesion. Healing involved the shaman drawing out the evil spirit that had invaded a victim's body and expelling it through their own. Shamans extended their range to use herbal cures and potions, magic tricks, divining, tooth pulling, bonesetting and the first psychosurgery—trepanning skulls— to release evil spirits. Trepanning, or drilling holes in skulls, was often done to relieve the fatal pressure from a subdural haematoma. These ancient tribes had excellent antiseptic procedures and the primitive surgeon proved adept at putting the hole in the right place on the skull.

The shaman not only warded off death, but participated in group activities such as hunting, ritualised killing and, later, warfare. These activities were conceived as sanctioned healing for a higher purpose. The life of the medicine man (or woman) was by no means easy; failing to get the prediction right could mean becoming the next sacrifice of the chief, headman or king.

Modern medicine has retained: the tendency to meet the needs of a hereditary or elite class before attending to the masses; receiving the hostility of patients or relatives to the failure to ward off disease and death; and, despite their elevated status, doctors are susceptible to being scapegoated at the perception of failure.

As humans moved from hunter–gatherer communities to agricultural settlements, a distinct shamanic class arose. This was often a skill that was passed down to male relatives, but it wasn't exclusively male. Suitable candidates were selected at a young age and tutored in their craft. Religion and society developed increasingly complex role specialisation but the shaman, in one form or another, continued to flourish.

Any reading of the Bible or Homer will confirm the status of prophets, healers and medicine men. New Testament exorcists, for example, operated by speech and touch. Jesus himself was a wandering healer and exorcist in the Galilean countryside, commanding evil spirits to leave the body of the afflicted person. Many of his patients had epilepsy or hysteria and, ironically, as his fame spread, his appearance at Galilean villages led to mass hysteria! The Gospels tell us that Jesus was constantly asked to heal the 'possessed', even though this may have interfered with his mission as a prophet. In the episode of the Gadarene swine, Jesus commands the demonic spirits to leave the tormented victim and go into the swine, causing the 200-strong herd to rush off the cliff into the lake and drown, leaving the riparian farmer most unimpressed, if not causing mayhem among the spectators. Even Jesus experienced the lack of gratitude from patients that healers have had to deal with since time immemorial.

In their death-defying capacity, doctors are the modern heirs of the shaman, witchdoctor, medicine man or healer. The medical profession dates back over two thousand years, with the first ethical principles laid down by the ancient Greek School of Hippocrates, and medical and surgical skills developed during the Arab era. However, much of what doctors did for their patients consisted of reheated ancient ideas, remedies or witchcraft, doing little more than giving a sense that something was being done.

Initially, there was no distinction between body and soul, or in more modern parlance, between mind and brain. In the West, souls, accompanied however reluctantly by their attendant bodies, were the province of the Catholic Church. The Church used doctors to extend its own power, thereby maintaining their exclusivity. At the height of the Spanish witch persecutions in the fourteenth century, doctors were mandated by the Church to examine suspects and organise torture to get them to confess to heresy.

The Church's vice-like grip started to weaken with Renaissance discoveries of the structure and function of the body. Vesalius's work on anatomy and Harvey's discovery of the flow of blood were crucial in wresting medicine from the Church, putting it on the path to becoming a clinical science.

Descriptions by Spanish doctors of the first recorded episodes of syphilis in the late fifteenth century, for example, reveal good skills in observing disease.

Despite these developments, medicine remained a fiercely contested domain. The eighteenth century was the high time of the 'quack'. Quacks mostly came from marginal groups, such as Jews and gypsies, who depended on their initiative to get established. They were assiduous self-promoters, made sure they got to where the clients were and, in many cases, were a lot cheaper than doctors. Widely derided by doctors, quacks often led their medical colleagues who would then steal the remedies for their own use.

The distance between doctor and patient reflected the times. Until 150 years ago, doctors did little more than talk and hold a pulse, doling out medicine that was patently ineffective. Rene Laennec, unusually for a Frenchman, objected to having to put his ear on the unwashed but perfumed breasts of his female patients, so he invented the stethoscope, providing an objective distance between doctor and patient.

Somewhere during the time of Queen Victoria, all this changed. As medicine became scientific, the distance between doctor and patient vanished. It was a revolutionary step when the suitably diffident Royal Obstetrician, his head turned away, tentatively inserted a hand under the Royal Gown to perform a vaginal examination during Her pregnancy. From that time, no orifice was safe from invasion, regardless of embarrassment, discomfort or distaste.

For all the posturing about ancient medical colleges, the official recognition of doctors is a nineteenth-century phenomenon. Although it now seems an accepted fact that medicine and surgery are amalgamated, this was by no means the case in the past. Three different medical groups existed, competed and variously claimed to be superior and professionally ethical: physicians, surgeons and apothecaries. Alongside these bodies competed a range of other groups: quacks, charlatans, healers, tooth pullers, manipulators and massagers, herbalists and soothsayers.

Technology, population surges and fear of change led to a need for control and regulation. This manifested with the institutionalisation of police work, border controls and internal regulation of professions and trades. By 1900, the registration of doctors was an established fact in most countries, including the United States. The legitimisation of professional status was followed by the formalisation of medical training and qualification rules. In the United States, this required the Flexner Report to revolutionise the profession and ensure that medical schools were not hole-in-the-wall operations issuing fake licences, a regular practice in many states in the past.

The development of specialisation facilitated the rise of medical status. This started in France after 1820, no surprise in view of the domination of French medicine in the age of Pinel. The French had greater numbers of doctors associated with hospitals and teaching centres with organised health care—not for nothing is the word *bureaucrat* derived from that period. The British preference for generalists rather than specialists and resistance from the medical establishment meant it took them far longer to make these changes. However, political pressure led to the institutionalisation of obstetrics and, after the 1880s, there was an inexorable path to specialisation.

Regulation of the medical profession tended to be erratic and inconsistent at first. There was a wide gap between promise and practice, allowing many exemptions to flourish or exploit the rules. Non-medical practitioners were never outlawed, for example. Departments of Health did not exist.

Medical scandals led to public outcries and more government promises to regulate medical practice. Consequently, it was not until well into the 1920s in most countries that it could be said that a medical doctor was someone who had completed formal training, supervision and requirements.

The onset of the twentieth century coincided with growth in cities, population surges, movement of people, technological development and the clash between empires. The golden century of medicine promised no end of developments that could hold back the tyranny of disease and prolong life, seemingly endlessly.

Specialities were expanding their range, especially within surgery, and hospitals became diagnostic and surgical centres. Medical schools with their adjoining teaching hospital were great centres of research and treatment, creating an environment that was inspiring, dedicated, reifying or alternately dehumanising, alienating and mechanistic.

With medical power came technological changes. For the first time, the promise of curing human ailments with drugs appeared to be a reality. Chloral hydrate came into use as a sleeping agent in 1869, followed by sulphonal in 1888, only to be trumped by the first of the barbiturates, Veronal, in 1903. These drugs were highly potentiated, powerful in producing sedation, sleep and analgesia, and all highly addictive. Pharmacology provided effective drugs to treat the ancient scourges of syphilis and tuberculosis. By 1905, the syphilis organism had been identified, in 1910 Salvarsan 606 offered an alternative to mercury treatment, and Wagner Juarreg developed malarial fever treatment in 1917.

Drugs required a new means of administration: the syringe. First used two centuries earlier, improvements to the syringe in 1856 made the administration of potent drugs a reality. This coincided with the refinement of opium into morphine, a product of great potency that could not only provide rapid relief of pain but just as easily kill by respiratory arrest with a minute increase in dose. Anyone who doubts this need only walk through old cemeteries with their sad little tombstones announcing that this baby or child passed 'into sleep', inadvertently killed by the very nostrum intended to soothe or placate them. In 1898 morphine was trumped by the development of diacetylmorphine, also called diamorphine but known to the world as heroin, an even more refined opiate, and exquisitely narcotic. Demonstrating how technological advances in medicine invariably led to new problems, the rise in the use of potent narcotics administered by syringe caused an exponential increase in narcotic addiction.

As medical power was being institutionalised, the need for more technological development became insatiable, leading to the development of the great chemical and pharmaceutical companies. In the words of Roy Porter: 'Medicine was good for business and business was good for medicine.'

After World War II, medicine was on the edge of an era of undreamed-of promise. The discovery of penicillin implied an end to infectious diseases, new ethical rules were introduced on human experimentation and burgeoning technology had the potential to make life, if not infinite, at least a lot longer and safer. Some, but not all, of this promise was realised. Developments in public health, nutrition, surgery, pharmacology and diagnosis converted many conditions from lethal to merely disruptive or, at worst, chronic ailments that could be lived with. Infectious diseases did indeed cease to kill the young, the old, the weak and the immunologically compromised. But antibiotics, it turned out, promoted bacterial resistance and began to lose their effectiveness. Furthermore, the wonders of First World antibiotics translated poorly to the Third World, where limited access to modern medical care was only one element in a Hobbesian scenario of poor nutrition, sanitation, hygiene and poverty.

As medical therapeutics and technology advanced, disease merely retreated, realigned and emerged in new forms, usually as chronic illness, environmental ailments and the resurgence of some infectious diseases. There had barely been time to declare smallpox extinct when AIDS emerged, apparently out of the jungles of Africa. With it returned ancient scourges like syphilis, tuberculosis and a host of other infections, now antibiotic resistant.

Disease became chronic, rather than acute. The focus of treatment became degenerative conditions, especially in an aging population that had never survived in such large numbers in the past. This brought a new flood of problems in its wake. Doctors are trained to treat acute conditions; after all, what did not kill you, made you stronger. Now they had to treat patients who remained in various stages of unwellness, creating hitherto unheard of states such as the 'very old elderly', an inconceivable concept in an earlier time when an influenza epidemic could kill with pneumonia in three days.

This situation is illustrated by the concept of *clinical life*: a life that only exists as a result of highly technical interventions such as coronary artery bypass grafts. The denizens of clinical life live in a state of virtual reality, haunted by a single immutable fact: no such intervention can ever succeed in providing what is hoped for. Clinical life can never meet the desire for an endless, painless, death-free existence. Imposing this expectation on a reality-based doctor can only result in dismay, disdain and dissolution.

The current view of illness, and how and who deals with it, is a reflection of our post-industrial scientifically focused and individual-orientated world. In the fourteenth century, if a woman behaved strangely she could be declared to be a witch by church authorities. In the nineteenth century (and, indeed, most of the first half of the twentieth century), masturbation was regarded as a cause of insanity, if not many other ailments. For the first half of the twentieth century, it was not accepted that a naughty child who kept making faces could have the complications of rheumatic fever. For decades, cigarettes were advertised in medical journals as health promoting. Now there are intense debates over the validity of newly defined conditions like fibromyalgia, allergy to the twentieth century, Munchausen syndrome by proxy and chronic fatigue syndrome, regarded by some as new manifestations of hysteria brought into the medical market place as a result of pressure by lobby groups, rather than scientific recognition of a clinical syndrome. Others see the refusal to accept these conditions as legitimate diseases as evidence of a conspiracy by medicine, representing the establishment, to deny them recognition as deserving patients.

At the same time, we see the phenomenon of disease-mongering by pharmaceutical companies and other lobby groups. Routine events of life, such as menopause, waning sexual potency, obesity and—worst of all—grieving over the loss of a loved one, have been converted into medical or psychiatric 'disorders', meaning they can seek approval for distribution or funding of expensive drugs developed for this purpose.

Pharmaceutical companies are by no means the only offenders. Consider the legitimisation of post-traumatic stress disorder (PTSD). War neurosis, under a guise of different labels, is as old as warfare, morphing into different manifestations over the ages, varying with circumstance and culture. The legitimisation of PTSD, however, resulted from political lobbying by the Viet Nam Veterans' Association in the United States, hardly a scientific process.

The penalty paid for modern medicine is the fantastic complexity of health care systems, the majority of which struggle under budgetary constraints; the denizens within, workers and patients, lost in a giant Kafkaesque ant colony. Communism may have died in Eastern Europe, but Marx's pointed comment about surplus value labour alienated from control of resources is most apposite. As medical technology developed, the gap widened further. Why would a doctor prod and poke around to make what was at best a subjective finding when it is easier and safer (from a malpractice point of view) to send a patient off for a scan, scope or test of some sort?

A good example of this are the CT and MRI scans, now routinely used for a wide range of conditions. Scanning involves sending the patient on a movable trolley into a small tunnel surrounded by the scanner machinery, resembling a giant cement mixer. This causes such distress on occasion that it is now routine to check whether patients are claustrophobic, anxious or agitated, in which case scanning is done under sedation.

Technology is dehumanising and the gap between doctor and patient has widened to a chasm in which the human element is reduced to a faint whisper barely heard above the whirl of scanners, the beeping of monitor screens and the buzzing of centrifuges. Users of medical services are told that they are no longer passive patients, blindly following the commands of a godlike doctor; they are instead consumers, with a Charter of Rights, expectations and entitlements, a situation which could only arise in the minds of ideologues who perceive illness as another commodity to be regulated in a capitalist society.

This created the greatest crisis in the history of medicine. Medicine had always been a calling to an elevated profession. This included the acquisition of a special knowledge, responsibilities and self-regulation. The modern doctor is expected to master a range of skills that impose intense pressures on the doctor, whether in general or specialist practice. This is aptly summed up by psychiatrist John Romano:

> Is the clinician a biochemist, a biophysicist, a biologist, a pathologist, a psychologist, a psychiatrist, a social scientist, a statistician? In my view, he is none of these and at the same time he must be something of all of them.

In the process, the mystique, allure and aura of medicine suffered a fatal blow. Doctors are now mere 'providers' who can be regulated like any other group, their territory invaded by competitors like nurses, psychologists or, worst of all, 'alternative practitioners'—the enemy truly is at the gates.

There are any number of self-interested agents, regulatory and legal, to urge patients to complain, sue and seek redress. We live in the culture of complaint. There is no finer terrain for indignation, loathing and strident sanctimony than the embattled field of health care, despite the fact that we are living longer, better and easier, constantly benefiting from phenomenal advances in surgical science. As all life, no matter how saintly, ends in death, physicians are held to an impossible ideal. Medical practice is always a matter of possibilities and probabilities, but in the age of the informed consumer, egged on by a tabloid culture ever poised to go into a feeding frenzy to highlight scandal, the medical profession has gone into a defensive crouch from which it has yet to emerge and it is clear that the ancient doctor–patient relationship has been distorted beyond recognition.

2

Twentieth-century clinicide
Dr Marcel Petiot's course of medical mayhem

The 'highest' states of mind held up before mankind by
Christianity as of supreme value, are actually forms of
convulsive epilepsy.

Friedrich Nietzsche

Occupied Paris: On 21 March 1944, police and fire authorities
were called to the Paris home of Dr Marcel Petiot when
neighbours were disturbed by a thick pall of smoke and
revolting odour emanating from the residence. When they
entered, the police found a charnel house of decomposing
human body parts. The kitchen was designed as a mortuary
with a dissecting table and pipe leading directly into the sewer

to dispose of waste. Outside the house were lime pits filled with human remains. As they were wandering through the necropolis, their minds struggling to comprehend what they saw, Petiot arrived on his bicycle.

Unconcerned by the arrival of the authorities, Petiot told the police that he was in the Resistance and the bodies were those of Germans whom he had to kill to ensure the secrecy of his operation to smuggle refugees and Resistance agents out of the country. The oppressive rule of the Nazis was at its height, so the French police followed their patriotic sense and chose to believe this fantastic account. Petiot was advised to flee. Official investigations continued, revealing the remains of at least 86 cadavers, and the French police made sure they obstructed the investigating Germans as much as possible. Petiot went into hiding, only emerging after the liberation of Paris and joining the Free French Forces (as did most of the French population), claiming to be a Resistance hero who had killed 63 collaborators. He was soon arrested and went to trial on 18 March 1946.

Marcel André Félix Petiot was born on 17 January 1897 at Auxerre, France. He was raised by an aunt and grew up in comfortable surroundings. Highly intelligent, he was already showing alarming behaviour during childhood. Obsessed with books about murder, he had a penchant for torturing animals, and by the age of twelve he had been examined for problems due to bedwetting, epilepsy and sleepwalking. He made passes at male classmates and collected knives and guns.

When he was fifteen, Petiot's mother died. His behaviour worsened, and he displayed signs of kleptomania. To no one's surprise, he was expelled from school many times. In 1914, a psychiatrist determined that 'personal and hereditary problems' absolved him from responsibility for his actions, which resulted in allowing him to finish his education in a special academy in Paris in July 1915.

In January 1916, Petiot was drafted into the French infantry. He was wounded and gassed at Aisne and had a mental breakdown. He was sent to various asylums, was arrested for stealing army blankets and jailed in Orleans. In a psychiatric hospital at Fleury-les-Aubrais he was again diagnosed as being mentally ill but, in view of the military crisis, returned to the front in June 1918. He was transferred three weeks later after he shot himself in the foot, and was attached to a new regiment in September, but did not last long before ending up back in the psychiatric hospital. In 1919, Petiot was discharged from military service as unfit due to 'neurasthenia, amnesia, mental unbalance, sleepwalking, severe depression, paranoia and suicidal tendencies'. This got him a 40 per cent disability pension, increased the following year to 100 per cent when a government psychiatrist confirmed that he could not do physical or intellectual work.

Undeterred by a chaotic history some may have perceived as an impediment to regular employment, let alone practising medicine, Petiot entered the accelerated program for war veterans, completing medical school in eight months and then completing an internship. He received his medical degree in December 1921, having trained in Evreux Mental Hospital where he had been previously confined with a diagnosis of dementia praecox (as schizophrenia was then known). After 1923, although still having seizures, his disability pension was halved.

Petiot set up a medical practice at Villeneuve-sur-Yonne, where he charged patients for services that were already paid for by government medical assistance funds. When he started at Villeneuve-sur-Yonne, Petiot seemed restrained and withdrawn; he was using narcotics heavily. His only interest was a sports car that he drove in a manic fashion, having many accidents. He was probably having fits while driving or was under the influence of drugs. Another oddity noticed by the townspeople was his kleptomania, with him continually stealing small, largely unwanted items.

Petiot's first victim seems to have been Louise Delaveau, the daughter of a patient, with whom he had an affair in 1926. After she disappeared, neighbours said they had seen Petiot load a trunk into his car. Police investigated the case, but dismissed Delaveau as a runaway.

In 1927, Petiot married Georgette Lablais and their son, Gerhardt, was born the next year. Petiot then ran for mayor of the town, hiring an accomplice to disrupt his opponent's campaign, and won the election. Although Petiot's behaviour in office was characterised by blatant theft and corruption, he had a magical hold on the village electorate. After he was suspended as a mayor in August 1931, the council resigned in sympathy, and within five weeks he was elected as Yonne District Councillor. But it wasn't long before he was accused of stealing electric power and he lost his seat the following year.

Deprived of his political base and sensing that past misdemeanours were likely to catch up with him, Petiot moved to Paris and set up a practice at 66 Rue Caumartin, making exaggerated claims of his qualifications and skills. In 1936 he was appointed Médecin D'état-Civil with the authority to write death certificates. He soon attracted patients, along with repeated rumours of performing illegal abortions and prescribing addictive medication. A woman he had operated on in his rooms later died at home. She was found to have a large amount of morphine in her body, but no action was taken.

In 1936, Petiot's kleptomania got him into trouble when he was detained after he stole a book. He was legally committed to a psychiatric hospital in a disturbed and paranoid state, but managed to arrange a transfer to a private institution. There he easily convinced the director he was sane and was examined by three leading psychiatrists. Despite finding that Petiot was utterly immoral, without scruples and mentally unbalanced, they decided there were no legal grounds to hold him.

In 1941, Petiot bought a house at 21 Rue le Sueur. Adopting the codename of 'Dr Eugène', he developed a false escape route, known as Fly-Tox, claiming he could arrange safe passage through Portugal to Argentina for Jews, Resistance fighters or criminals. He accepted anyone who could pay 25,000 francs. His aides Raoul Fourrier, Edmond Pintard and René-Gustave Nézondet funnelled the victims to him. People who trusted him to deliver them to safety were never seen alive again. He injected victims with cyanide, took their valuables and disposed of the bodies in the Seine, submerged them in quicklime or incinerated them.

Petiot's trial in 1946 was a sensation in post-war Paris, attracting journalists, the rich and the famous. It revealed how Petiot exploited every person or institution he dealt with, including the army, medical school, hospitals, doctors, pharmacists, and political, government and tax officials as well as police and military officers. While the outcome seemed inevitable, Petiot was not disconcerted in the slightest by the court, constantly over-ruling his lawyers and making sardonic outbursts in response to any statement critical of him. He conducted a vigorous defence, following his lifetime pattern of continuously fabricating stories to explain every allegation against him. He had no compunction about screaming abuse at witnesses or causing chaos in the court. At other times, he seemed bored and indifferent. The story of running a clandestine Resistance operation to eliminate Gestapo suspects was soon exposed. There was no evidence that Petiot had ever been in the Resistance.

Found guilty, Petiot was sentenced to death by guillotine. Just before he was about to ascend the platform, he requested a delay to empty his bladder. The executioner commented that he had never seen a condemned man with such indifference to death.

From a psychiatric point of view, Petiot is almost impossible to categorise. He had many hospital admissions and was diagnosed with schizophrenia, manic depression, paranoia and psychopathy. Although he had affairs and raped victims, he did not seem greatly interested in sex as an adult, in contrast to making passes at boys at school. That he was completely lacking in remorse is beyond doubt; he was also utterly convincing when he wanted to be, as testified by many patients and constituents who spoke of him in glowing terms. At times Petiot was depressed, agitated, confused or psychotic. Yet these states could not have lasted very long and it seems impossible that someone with schizophrenia could have been as organised as he was. Equally so, it seems doubtful that he could have had prolonged episodes of mania without it being obvious to people around him.

Petiot displayed other pathological phenomena, such as kleptomania, pseudologia fantastica (the telling of fantastic tales and lies) and seizures. These problems most probably arose from a neuropsychiatric condition. The likely cause was brain damage, either from a birth injury or childhood infection, causing TLE (temporal lobe epilepsy). TLE is associated with severe personality changes, psychosis, obsessional behaviour and bizarre sexual practices in some cases.

Guillotining, unfortunately, not being conducive to post-mortem brain examination, meant we shall never know what pathological processes affected Petiot's thinking and behaviour. What we do know is that Petiot's murderous career was conducted in the course of his career as a doctor, using the medical skills that were intrinsic to the profession. Charming, mendacious, morally bankrupt, mentally disturbed, lascivious and utterly indifferent to the trail of mutilated corpses that he left in his wake, Petiot served as a role model for the clinicide that followed in the rest of the twentieth century. His case shows how clinicide overlaps with serial killing, a phenomenon that took off at the end of the nineteenth century. Petiot became the first medical serial killer of the twentieth century, but he was by no means the last. After his judicial dispatch in 1946, there were some who may have thought that Petiot was a one-off aberration. As will be shown, this hope sadly was not to be realised.

3

Neurosurgeon with a needle

Dr Michael Swango

This is the story of America. Everybody's doing what they think they're supposed to do.

Jack Kerouac, *On the Road*

A patient lies in bed, recovering from routine surgery. When the intravenous drip stops running, the nurse calls the resident to the room. The doctor, tall, blond and good-looking, seems noncommittal, bending over the mess of tubes, cannulas and fluid taps, fussing with the connections. He glances over his shoulder at the lingering nurse, seeming annoyed that she is watching. The nurse leaves, wondering why he is taking so long over a matter that involves no more than flushing out the administration valve of the drip line.

When the door closes, the doctor glances briefly at the patient; the patient observes that he is unusually intense, almost pent-up in anticipation. In a swift movement, the doctor discards the saline syringe taken from the drip tray, and almost too quickly to follow, removes a syringe hidden in the top pocket of his white coat. Before the patient can comprehend what is happening, the syringe is connected to the valve, which is opened and flushed through with a coloured liquid, swirling briefly in the clear saline of the tube.

The doctor turns away rapidly, the used syringe swept impatiently into his pocket, glancing back at the patient with an odd sneering look.

'Goodbye,' he seems to mutter. The patient's world suddenly goes black, a huge shuddering breath is exhaled and he knows no more.

Serial killing is the hallmark of the psychopath, a character incapable of remorse, lacking empathy for other people's feelings and driven solely by the desire to reward his or her own needs. What is not recognised is that there are varying degrees of psychopathy and some individuals combine a high intelligence with an ability to manipulate others to advance their career. A certain degree of ruthlessness, after all, is no handicap in climbing the academic or clinical ladder, and the authoritarian and hierarchical nature of medicine is nothing but encouraging for the career development of such individuals.

However, unleashed psychopathic drives can easily turn to seeking the ultimate sensation for emotionally numb individuals: the power over life and death, the all-too-frequent opportunities provided by medicine to usurp this power for personal thrill—first by chance, then by experimentation, finally by compulsion to re-experience a sensation that requires constant killing.

Michael Swango was unreservedly psychopathic, possessing in abundance qualities such as lack of remorse, glib self-confidence, indifference to the feelings of others, low frustration tolerance, preoccupation with extreme violent and sadistic fantasies, and intense hedonism. It can be said with some certainty that no one at his medical school had truly known Swango during his years as an undergraduate or in the Marines. His behaviour as a student did attract attention, but it was laughed off. When he began killing as an intern, the authorities refused to believe it and he was allowed to continue. In contrast to Dr Harold Shipman, who presented himself as a mild-mannered and caring doctor, Swango never made any effort to hide his necrophiliac[1] obsessions and, in retrospect, the warning signs were there from an early stage.

Like many serial killers, Swango modelled himself on his predecessors; he would keep scrapbooks about murderers and torturers. The obsession with murder and violent death was pervasive; he could scarcely keep from talking about the subject, obtaining gory reading material and watching gruesome movies. He was extraordinarily glib, persuasive and without any restraint in misleading or manipulating people to suit his ends.

The man who was to be one of America's worst serial killers was born Joseph Michael Swango,[3] but he dropped the first name at an early age. His father, Colonel Virgil Swango, a career army officer, did four tours in Vietnam. The family moved to sixteen different military bases during Michael's upbringing. When he was home, Virgil Swango was authoritarian and strict with his three boys, insisting they line up in military order for inspection. He was a heavy drinker and the marriage broke up, although the couple never divorced. He spent the last years of his life in a mobile home, dying of cirrhosis of the liver, embittered about the treatment of veterans.

Virgil Swango was deeply interested in violence. He kept scrapbooks of clippings about murder, arson and violent crime, a surprising interest for a Vietnam veteran; many soldiers had returned from Vietnam with post-traumatic stress disorder and would do everything possible to avoid scenes of brutality that brought back memories of combat experiences.

Robert Swango, the eldest son, described the family home as emotionally starved. His father was always on duty in Vietnam and his mother, Muriel, was distant. He and brother John, two years younger than Michael, left home at an early age. As the only son to go to university, Michael was clearly his mother's favourite, but it is unlikely he did much to respond to her affection except in the most nominal way.

A bright student, musically talented and a track champion, Michael was popular with fellow students at Catholic Boys High School in Quincy, Illinois. Blond-haired and blue-eyed, he had no difficulty attracting girls. He volunteered to work for the Republican Party in Quincy, putting him at odds with brother Robert, a leading figure in the local anti-war movement. Swango dominated his senior yearbook—valedictorian, band president, National Merit Scholarship finalist. Voted 'Most Likely to Succeed' (which he did, except in the most perverse and appalling way), he aspired to be a marine.

Swango studied music at Millikin University College, was polite and studious and, unlike his classmates, did not go partying, demonstrating, or participating in protests. However, after a romance ended in his second year, he started wearing military garb, painted his car army green and began a scrapbook of news-paper clippings of car and plane crashes, military coups, sex crimes, arson and riots. Dropping out of college, Swango signed up for the US Marines. He left Camp Lejeune, North Carolina, with an honourable discharge in 1976, returning to Quincy College to obtain a degree to get into medical school. Working after-hours as an ambulance attendant at a medical centre, Swango got high grades. His senior-year thesis was a detailed examination of an unusual and, in retrospect, highly significant topic: the murder of Bulgarian dissident Gregory Markov. A rebel whom the communist authorities wished to eliminate, Markov was stabbed with an umbrella tip in a crowded London street, implanting a tiny pellet of ricin, a highly toxic and previously unknown poison manufactured by the KGB, an organisation with considerable expertise in these matters. (Swango later tried to manufacture ricin and it is suspected he used it in some poisonings.)

Accepted into Southern Illinois University Medical School, Swango immediately attracted the attention of fellow students with his strange behaviour. He blatantly flaunted test rules, running outside the examination hall to scan textbooks (which led to the rules being changed after a professor complained about 'Swango-ing'). In one instance, he presented his anatomical dissection study, displaying a hacked-up mess of tissue. On another occasion, he did not recognise a basic human feature: the outline of a heart in an X-ray. Yet he seemed indifferent to criticism and kept to himself.

Swango's behaviour continued to draw notice during his clinical terms. This is the time when medical trainees are allocated patients to examine and write up, known as clerkship. He was called '007—Licence to Kill' by students because of the frequency that his clerking patients died; it struck no one at the time that this could be non-accidental, nor was anyone alarmed that he seemed to relish writing in big letters on patient files that the patient had DIED.

In 1982, his final year at medical school, Swango's father died, an event that left him unmoved as they had not been in contact for years. Yet the two had a bizarre posthumous bond. His mother gave him a scrapbook she found among his father's personal effects. It was similar to the one Michael was already keeping but more detailed, a collection of news clippings and photographs of disasters, from assassinations to mass killings. When he saw the scrapbook, Swango is reported to have said that his dad couldn't have been so bad after all.

Indifferent to any rules, Swango often disappeared or showed up late for clerking duties. His obstetrics/gynaecology supervisor reported him after he faked case reports on patients he had not examined. As a result, he failed the rotation and was not allowed to graduate with the rest of the class. Typically, he did not tell his mother, who was left waiting for him to arrive at a graduation party.

Swango repeated the course, this time successfully and applied for a position as an intern. His 'Dean's letter', essential for the application, documented the poor impression he had made as a medical student. Despite this handicap, Swango's luck held and he was accepted at Ohio State University Medical Center for an internship in general surgery, followed by a neurosurgery residency.

Swango was delighted to get a chance to achieve his ambition to be a neurosurgeon. Why neurosurgery? It is one of the most intricate disciplines, operating in the high-risk territory of the brain, requiring a combination of extreme skill and preparedness to take risks. Because of the nature of the work, neurosurgeons tend to be detached and highly technically minded; it would be difficult to cope otherwise. Neurosurgical patients are often seriously injured, in a comatose state, or requiring intensive care; a high mortality rate is expected with these patients. The appeal to a risk-seeker such as Swango, who relished blood and gore, is obvious.

Swango's behaviour as an intern was no different than when at medical school. If chastised at ward rounds, he would fall to the ground and do push-ups as if he were a marine on parade. Although it was against hospital regulation, he moonlighted as an ambulance worker, adding to an already overstrained workload. It seems unlikely he needed the money, so it is probable the job provided access to drugs and fed his fantasies by providing him with ample contact with severely injured patients.

Joan Credeur was the property manager at Harvard Square in Upper Arlington, where Swango lived during his internship. In a newspaper interview she revealed that Swango's one-bedroom apartment was spartan, with a sofa and chairs but no bed. He kept newspapers piled up, but the apartment wasn't dirty. Whenever he saw Credeur, she recalled, Swango went out of his way to greet her.

'His first Christmas there, he even gave me a present; he gave me candy. I couldn't eat it because I'm allergic to chocolate, but other people ate it, and we didn't have any sick people here,' she said. 'He could have sold a refrigerator to an Eskimo. He had that baby face, nice appearance, and he was always immaculate. There was nothing that would give a clue what he was really like.'

On the morning of 31 January 1984, Swango entered the room of Ruth Barrick to check on her intravenous line. The attending nurse, Deborah Kennedy, thought this strange as routine checks had been performed earlier by residents, not interns. Returning to the room twenty minutes later, she found Swango gone but the patient had turned blue and was suffocating. Rigorous efforts to resuscitate the patient followed. She recovered in intensive care, leaving doctors puzzled at what had caused the respiratory failure.

Barrick's daughter, Louella Carnahan, thought that Swango was a model of a caring doctor who would put his arm around her and tell her that her mother was going to be fine.

The following night, student nurse Karolyn Beery checked on patient Rena Cooper who was recovering from a back operation. She saw Swango injecting something into the intravenous line with a syringe. He said nothing and walked out, and several moments later the patient began choking and turning blue. The resuscitation team worked on her and within fifteen minutes her colour returned. While unable to speak, Cooper scribbled a note that someone had given her something in the IV which caused paralysis.

The nurse reported the matter but the hospital administration was reluctant to believe that Swango had done this intentionally. This is no surprise. The idea that a doctor would allow himself to be witnessed deliberately injecting a seriously ill patient would strike most people as highly unlikely. Furthermore, that he assisted in the resuscitation made the accusation seem even more far-fetched. Institutions being institutions, the (male) administrators would have been well aware of the status imbalance between accused and accuser; the former a plausible and articulate male doctor, the latter not just an unqualified nurse, but female.

The matter passed through several impromptu committees; numerous consultants conducted peremptory inquiries. Weighing heavily over the investigation was the hospital's fear of being sued if they could not prove that Swango had knowingly harmed the patients. It was decided there was no basis for the claims. Years later when the cases were again investigated, it seemed that the investigating doctors, all senior and male, decided Swango was innocent without examining the facts, dismissing the mostly female witnesses as unreliable. Institutional stasis and nepotism aside, this is a common response to such deaths when it seems inconceivable that a doctor could deliberately kill patients.

Untouched by the claims, there was no impediment to Swango continuing with his internship and he duly proceeded to the next rotation at Rhodes Hall, another unit in the hospital. His arrival there was associated with an unusual increase in patient deaths—more in a few weeks than there had been for the entire year. In each case, the patient had been doing well and had not been diagnosed with a life-threatening illness. Six others included nineteen-year-old gymnast Cynthia Ann McGee who was found dead in her bed on 14 January 1984; 21-year-old Richard DeLong who died unexpectedly on 21 January 1984; and 47-year-old Rein Walker who also passed away without warning. Dorothy Zielienski, a practical nurse who worked on the neurosurgery wing, noted that an alarming number of patients were suddenly critical. 'We were used to having one or two "Code Blues" a year, and then in one week we had nine,' Zielienski said.

Swango was seen acting strangely at or near the room of each of these patients, but he was never questioned about this. Otherwise, Swango kept to himself, walking around with his head down and rarely talking to others—even the nurse he was dating. Rita Dumas had met Swango after he arrived in Columbus and was attracted by his enthusiasm and energy. He even babysat her children on a regular basis.

Swango's next rotation was to be in surgery at Doan Hall. Once again, there was a sudden increase in unexplained deaths. Dr Ronald Ferguson, the director of transplant surgery, supervised Swango on rounds. 'For anybody looking at a herd of white coats, he wouldn't have stood out,' he said. 'He certainly was not some weirdo slinking around the hospital. He could be anything he wanted to be. I saw him being incredibly charming or going into his reclusive mode.'

But at times, Swango made strange comments. 'I recall him particularly talking about being a Green Beret in Vietnam during rounds one day. He talked very aggressively; I thought I was talking to John Wayne,' Ferguson said. In fact, Swango had never served in Vietnam or been a Green Beret.

The Residency Review Committee reviewed Swango's progress in February 1984. Apart from the suspicious deaths—at that stage deemed the subject of gossip—his performance was regarded as poor. One supervising doctor noted that he was preoccupied with Nazi history and the Holocaust. The university decided not to accept Swango as a resident when his internship ended in June.

Eventually deciding to follow the path of self-interest, the hospital administration made a deal with Swango. He would be given a reference to leave the hospital once he completed his internship, and no reports would be made to the authorities. Despite the cover-up, the Ohio State Medical Board, assessing Swango for a State Medical License, learned of his alleged link to patients' deaths. Surgical director Dr Larry Carey expressed misgivings about Swango, citing conflict with hospital staff and the Rena Cooper episode, but no one took notice, and in September 1984, the Board granted Michael Swango a licence to practise medicine in the State of Ohio.

Angry about the way he had been treated by the hospital administration, Swango returned to Quincy, telling his family that he had been a victim of a personality clash. Intending to seek a local medical licence, he was hired by the Adams County Ambulance Corps. Staff worked 24-hour shifts, sharing a suite of rooms in Blessing Hospital. Swango's co-workers were impressed by his medical knowledge but found him strange, detached and hyperactive: he spent his free time pasting clippings in his scrapbooks, and he constantly spoke about sex and violence, but laughed it off if questioned.

At this stage, Swango's modus operandi is evident. A number of people close to him experienced symptoms of poisoning, but no one died. It appears he used friends and co-workers as laboratory rats for poisoning experiments (mainly, but not exclusively, arsenic from rat poison), but killed patients in hospital with injections. These activities, in what was likely a revenge attempt for an imagined slight, came to a head when he fed arsenic-laden pizza to five ambulance staff.

His colleagues survived, but it was obvious Swango was responsible and the matter was passed on to the police. The Adams County sheriff searched Swango's apartment, uncovering a pile of vials, bottles, syringes and medical paraphernalia, in addition to a do-it-yourself weapon and murder manual. Handwritten poison recipes were found, as well as several handguns and knives. Swango was arrested and charged with seven counts of aggravated battery.

Swango's trial started in the Adams Country courthouse in Quincy on 22 April 1985. Prosecutors had learned of his history at Ohio State. Swango's defence was that he was accused on largely circumstantial evidence. He gave evidence and later spoke in mitigation before sentencing, portraying himself as a dedicated but misunderstood doctor, an unwitting victim of circumstances. Found guilty of poisoning the ambulance workers, Swango was sentenced to five years in jail at the Centralia Correctional Center. The conviction shattered his mother. She refused to pay for his appeal and severed ties with him.

In letters he wrote to a supporter from prison, Swango painted himself as a victim of appalling injustice committed by evil men. He refused to be examined by prison psychiatrists however, and in an attempt to gain public sympathy, he agreed to be interviewed for the *20/20* television program on 13 February 1986.

Insisting he was innocent of the charges, Swango said, 'I did not do these things. It is simply beyond my—well, beyond the sort of person I am to even think about doing something like that.' When the journalist told Swango the public feared his release from confinement, Swango responded: 'There's certainly no reason for anyone to be scared, none whatsoever.'

Swango did not have difficulties in jail; in fact, he was a model prisoner. After serving 30 months, he was paroled on good behaviour on 21 August 1987. He went to Hampton, Virginia, to serve out a year of probation with Rita Dumas, who had supported Swango during the trial and helped raise money for his appeal.

Rejected in his application for a medical licence in Virginia, Swango was hired as a work counsellor at the State Career Development Center but did not last long. His habit of working on his scrapbook at his desk caused some consternation. Other notable events were the complaint by one woman that he stalked her after she rejected his advances, and three colleagues going down with mysterious symptoms. His next position, as a lab technician at coal exporter Aticoal Services, lasted longer. He took courses to work as an emergency medical technician and married Rita on 8 July 1989. The marriage unravelled within 18 months, and it is likely that he poisoned her on at least one occasion, fortunately not fatally.

Despite serving a term in prison, Swango was determined to get back to medical practice as soon as possible. Exploiting the absence of a central register to check doctors' records and the reluctance of state boards to release information, he submitted a curriculum vitae with forged documents attesting to his outstanding work across the United States. The result? Swango was employed as an internist resident at Newport News Riverside Hospital in 1991. To explain the interruption to his medical career, he told the hospital that he had been jailed as the victim of a set-up. He convinced the hospital administrator that he was rehabilitated and was hired without any delay. Once again, his glib mendacity had overcome the odds to achieve his goals.

At Riverside, nurse Kristin Kinney, described as an attractive 26-year-old redhead, fell under his sway. She accepted Swango's tale that he was the fall guy in a bar-room brawl in which several people were hurt and he had taken all the blame. The couple got engaged but he was soon having affairs with other women. The engagement ended but there were a number of attempts at reconciliation. Kristin Kinney later died, allegedly a suicide, although the possibility that Swango poisoned her cannot be excluded.

Swango's practising rights were restored to him in Virginia, but he had no time to feel triumphant as press reports of his past soon surfaced. Always keen to intimidate anyone investigating him with the threat of litigation, he hired a lawyer to deal with the hospital authorities. This time it did not work and he was dismissed.

On the move again, in June 1993, Swango was accepted as a psychiatric resident at SUNY-Stonybrook, Long Island,

New York. He started as a resident in internal medicine at the Veterans Administration Hospital at Northport, Long Island, introducing himself as 'Dr Kirk', after the *Star Trek* television character. In no time he was back to his usual activities, leaving a trail of mysterious deaths in his wake. Again the media played a key role by publicising his past, and he had to resign.

Federal authorities were now on Swango's trail, tracing him to a friend's home near Atlanta, Georgia. They discovered he was working at a wastewater treatment facility connected to Atlanta's water supply. They obtained a warrant charging Swango with falsifying documents to work at the Veterans Administration Hospital. Before they could warn the local authorities of the threat, Swango made his biggest jump to date. He failed to appear at a hearing in August 1993 and had effectively vanished.

In 1994 Swango emerged in a most unlikely place: Bulawayo, Zimbabwe. Here he reinvented himself as a dedicated doctor disillusioned with the high-tech expensive medicine practised in the United States, wanting to help people in Africa. Polite, engaging, good-looking and sincere, he had no difficulty selling Swango *redividus* and won a position at a mission hospital. As his surgical skills were thought to be inadequate, he did a five-month internship at Mpilo Hospital in Bulawayo, where he worked with surgical resident Ian Lorimer. The men spent long periods together, and Lorimer noted that Swango frequently referred to Dostoevsky's *Crime and Punishment*. Swango would stay up all night and never complain about being tired.

In May 1995, Swango went to work at Mnene Mission Hospital in remote Mberengwa. His pleasant demeanour towards the staff did not last. He was inexplicably prone to wandering around the ward in the middle of the night, and before long, the killings started. A female patient, recovering from burns, suddenly collapsed and died for no evident reason. Patient Keneas Mzezewa was woken from sleep and given an injection by Swango, who curtly said goodbye as he walked away. Mzezewa was left paralysed and unconscious, but recovered to accuse Swango of injecting him. The nurses believed this, but did not want to take the matter further.

The deaths continued at a rapid and unprecedented rate. Swango seemed to be making less effort to hide his activities, either because he had less control over his impulses or he held the nurses in such contempt that he did not see them as a threat. The mortality rate rapidly escalated to a level that Dr Christopher Zshiri, the hospital director, could not ignore, and he called a meeting. He learned from a nurse that when Swango had been present at the bedside of a patient who died, he took a syringe out of his pocket and injected her. Dr Zshiri called the police, and an officer came to the hospital to investigate. He found a mess of syringes and equipment in Swango's room. Swango responded politely but denied any wrongdoing. He was suspended from duty and returned to Bulawayo, where he hired David Coltard, a leading civil rights lawyer, to defend him.

Investigations got nowhere. It was difficult to find proof, and the case stalled. In the interim, Swango persuaded the service to allow him to work without pay at Mpilo Hospital. A few deaths occurred but did not attract attention. Swango, however, appeared to be a changed character and attracted accolades for his work. His confidence rose sufficiently to mount a suit against his employers, the Lutheran Church, for repayment of lost wages. After eight months, it appeared the police investigation of the deaths at Mnene Hospital had trickled away. Just when it seemed Swango was in the clear, the investigation was mentioned in the press. The Minister of Health learned of the matter and Swango was dismissed.

By then he was living with his girlfriend, Lynette O'Hare, a white Zimbabwean. He dismissed rumours about the investigation on the grounds of jealousy and anti-white racism. Despite portraying himself as a devout Christian, he constantly spoke about violence, expressing interest in such exemplary role models as OJ Simpson and John Christie (the Ten Rillington Place murderer). Somewhat incongruously, he repeatedly watched the romantic comedy *Four Weddings and a Funeral*. Lynette O'Hare began to fear for her safety. She eventually asked Swango to leave, which he did, putting sugar in her car petrol tank as a parting gift. Finally, the net seemed to be closing. The police requested further interviews and Swango let people know that he was thinking of leaving the continent.

He disappeared from view but it turned out he had moved across the border to work in nearby Zambia. He had a position for two months as a physician at the University Teaching Hospital in Lusaka. News of an alert put out by the Zimbabwean authorities reached Lusaka, and he was barred from the hospital on 19 November 1996. Swango then surfaced in Johannesburg, South Africa, where he spent some months before getting a position at a hospital in Saudi Arabia. He passed through the United States on his way there but had to disembark on 27 June 1997 to renew a visa. At long last he was arrested when he tried to pass through customs.

Why did Swango disembark in Chicago under his own name knowing he could be detained by authorities? Had he reached a point where he needed an external intrusion to end his killing career and an announcement to the world of what he had achieved? Or was it a last opportunistic throw of the dice, loaded with the arrogance that he had got away with it thus far?

Charged with fraud on 12 July 1998 for falsifying his qualifications in 1991, Swango pleaded guilty and was given the maximum penalty of three years to be served at the high-security Sheridan Correctional Facility in Florence, Colorado. The authorities remained unaware of the full extent of his murderous career. Journalist James Stewart publicised the case, citing allegations that Swango had threatened to poison the city's water supply when he was set free. The news story sparked a renewed investigation, and a series of murder charges was prepared. In addition, Zimbabwe applied for his extradition to stand trial on five murder charges. Faced with the death penalty, Swango made a plea bargain in order to avoid pleading guilty to the three Long Island hospital murders, and was jailed for life.

At the trial, the prosecution cited his journal in which he had written of his pleasure at poisoning people in hospitals. He loved the 'sweet, husky, close smell of indoor homicide'. He claimed that murders were 'the only way I have of reminding myself that I'm still alive'. A major fatal accident was the ultimate fantasy. He loved coming out of the ER with an erection to tell parents their child was dead.

Swango will never be able to leave prison. Since sentencing, he has refused all requests for interviews and has effectively disappeared from the public eye, left to contemplate his necromantic memories for the rest of his life.

Swango always denied his guilt, presenting himself as a victim of injustice and media persecution. The denials, coupled with his plausible and convincing manner, persuaded people to overlook his past when he came out of jail in 1987 or, at the very least, not to investigate his compelling excuses.

He had no difficulty attracting women but soon lost interest, becoming remote and disconnected, and looking elsewhere. In at least two close relationships, he attempted to poison his partner, although it will never be known if he played any part in the death of Kristin Kinney. That Swango never killed his girlfriends or people he worked with by poisoning (although they were made extremely sick) would not have been accidental. These efforts were behavioural try-outs, trial runs to test the efficacy of the process and allow further scope for his fantasies. Another possibility is that, in a sadistic way, he rationalised this as a means of demonstrating his power, restraining himself from going as far as murder when he had a personal link with someone. It is not uncommon for serial murderers to mask or blindfold victims to dehumanise them before killing them. Patients, for Swango, could be perceived as anonymous, devoid of any feelings, only there to provide the unmatchable sexual thrill afforded by the power of rapidly killing them.

The symbolism of poisoning his victims with his injections should not be understated; as Swango's journal entries indicate, it was for him a sensation of intense potency, if not vitality. This is the clearest indication of the psychopathic affect: emotional blunting that can only be aroused by the most extenuated behaviour, invariably of an appalling, vile or violent nature.

4

Doctor as demiurge

Of all the professions, medicine is one most likely to attract people with high personal anxieties about dying. We become doctors because our ability to cure gives us power over the death of which we are so afraid.

Sherwin Nuland

Who is the doctor, and what factors in the profession of medicine facilitate the process of a doctor becoming a killer, rather than a healer?

Death is the central concern of human existence. When disease strikes, doctors stand between death and life. The tradition of the healer goes back to antiquity and invariably implies a special status: the demiurge. The demiurge was the classical deity responsible for the creation of the physical universe and the physical aspect of humanity. The deity principle implied a special privilege: exemption from the rules affecting common mortals. Death of course came to all, but the demiurge principle gave an exception to those so favoured. Doctors, notoriously difficult to treat, avoid the patient role by denial, neglect, self-diagnosis and self-treatment.

In studies that look at why people choose to become doctors, a constant finding is that healing the sick provides some insulation against the fear of death. This is why doctors are such awful patients, behaving alternately like potentates or children and refusing to comply with treatment. In a profession full of people trying to work out their own mortality, the appeal to a small number is to reverse the process: obtain immortality by killing the sick.

If doctors deny powerful needs in themselves, they can be either intolerant or compulsively solicitous of these in others, depending on patients for their self-esteem, worthiness and vicarious pleasure. But what if the dysfunction was excessive, unrecognised or pervasive? How would the doctor recognise and deal with it? Internalising feelings is an imperfect solution, and many doctors seek refuge in alcohol, drugs, dysfunctional relationships, depression, despair and ultimately suicide—the rate of suicide in medicine has always been higher than in other groups.

Starting with shamans and witchdoctors, through to psychological sages like Carl Jung, healers had to internalise their personal problems to function, using their personal experience to empathise with and assist their patients. Psychoanalyst Stanley Jackson developed the concept of the *Wounded Healer*. The *Wounded Healer complex* became prominent in organisations such as Alcoholics Anonymous and other self-help groups. This concept fitted in well with the psychoanalytic ethos that everyone was neurotic, and needed a good analysis to sort themselves out.

There is evidence that many people choose medicine because personal psychopathology makes them more vulnerable to stress—*the Helping Profession syndrome*. Some individuals go into medicine as a defence against feelings of helplessness or anxiety that have developed from an experience of illness in themselves or family members during childhood. The *Compulsive Care Giver* wants to give to others the care and attention they never received as a child. Psychoanalysts, never shy to see the worst in human nature, go a step further, referring to 'constructive vengeance': the unconscious desire to put right the wrongs of the past.

The medical school environment—as described by Charles Dickens—was always one of callousness and insensitivity. In 1840 William Dale wrote that 'drinking, smoking and brawling were the [regular] occupations of the dissecting room...' and it was not uncommon to see mock battles among the students using parts of the bodies as weapons. Something of this can also be gleaned from James Joyce, who knew about medical students, having preferred their companionship when he was a student at Trinity College.

In *Ulysses*, Stephen Dedalus stays in the Martello Tower with his nemesis, Buck Mulligan, a medical student. Haunted by the memory of his mother who recently died from cancer, Dedalus confronts Mulligan about his attitude, receiving the following reply:

> And what is death, he asked, your mother's or yours or my own? You saw only your mother die. I see them pop off every day in the Mater and Richmond and cut up into tripes in the dissecting room. It's a beastly thing and nothing else. It simply doesn't matter.

Doctors saw themselves as being one step away from gods, and it showed in their training and attitudes. Medical training gives little, if any, recognition of emotional reactions on the part of the doctor. Franz Kafka, who in his day job worked as a claims assessor for an insurance company, knew all about these sentiments.

In *Metamorphosis*, the horrifying story about transformation and reaction to illness, Gregor Samsa is transformed into a giant cockroach-like bug, provoking mixed reactions from his alarmed family. They come to believe that Samsa persecutes them, but they are renewed when he dies and they are 'rid of the thing'. The story is a reminder that each encounter with a patient inexorably changes the doctor, and not always for the better.

Training as a doctor means subduing the normal responses to pain, suffering, distress, coping with the mess and slop of indigent humans and handling tissues, organs and corpses in an indifferent fashion. A central rite of passage in medical training is the dissection of corpses and attending autopsies. This is not just a learning exercise, but a desensitising process.

From the start of medical training, ensuring a regular supply of undamaged corpses was a constant problem for the medical colleges. In the nineteenth century, the College of Surgeons in London received the bodies of those hanged for murder (it was seen as a further punishment for offenders). In Edinburgh, William Burke and William Hare developed something of a murder assembly line, known as burking, to provide unmarked corpses for Dr Robert Knox's anatomy school.[1]

There seemed to be no limits to what medicine could achieve, and the status and appeal of the profession continued to escalate. That medicine offered the opportunity to earn a reasonable living, if not become rich, did not escape the attention of future doctors. After World War II, the God principle intensified, and eventually, the numbers of medical schools and doctors rose to meet the growing demand. This produced a demographic change in the cosy middle-class old-school-tie environment of the medical school. With such large numbers of trainees and a wider selection criteria, it was inevitable that doctors would be drawn from all classes and backgrounds. All to the good, it would seem, to better relate to their patients, but one issue was not considered.

In the past, coming from a medical family, as so often happened, and going to the same schools, it was difficult to avoid being a known quantity as a medical student. Now, someone could go through medical school and graduate as a doctor without being personally known to anyone else in their class, and any strange or psychopathic personality traits would only show up later—perhaps too late—when they were exploring a desire to kill their hapless patients.

The impaired doctor uses his own psychopathology as a guide to helping patients with varying degrees of success. In far too many cases, this mental manoeuvre fails and they become overwhelmed in various ways. Denial of illness in colleagues is rife throughout the profession. Doctors may have difficulty in working with colleagues, patients, their relatives or other agencies, but it can go unreported. This results from unrecognised personal and institutional rivalry in individuals with a neurotic investment in the caring role.

Love, it seems, can coexist very closely with anger, if not hate, in the healing relationship. Like the police and army, doctors are taught to put aside unpleasant feelings until later, then to ignore them. Freud and his followers, for example, became infuriated at the temerity of some patients who refused to recover according to the predictions of psychoanalysis, referring to them as malignant or repulsive hysterics. Two such patients were Fraulein *Anna O.* (Bertha Pappenheim) and *Dora* (Ida Bauer), receiving for their pains decades of abuse in psychoanalytic literature.

This difficulty with ungrateful, rancorous or just plain unpleasant patients is a recurrent theme in medical writing. Several decades ago Leonard Heston wrote a famous paper on 'Dealing with the hateful patient'. Others followed with 'Taking a history from the difficult patient?', 'Impossible consultation made possible?', 'Doctor, why are you so detached?' and 'Personality Disorder: The patients psychiatrists dislike'. These papers, written in a lofty, elevated psychological fashion, reflected the underlying anxiety of doctors in practice, expressing the theme of 'We may have some problems of our own, but there are some bad mothers out there!'

Acerbic medical commentator Theodore Dalrymple quotes, with approval, the writing of Edinburgh physician Dr John Brown (1810–82). In his essay entitled 'The doctor—our duties to him' are listed the four duties of a patient: trust your doctor, obey your doctor, speak the truth to your doctor, and reward your doctor.

Dr Brown illustrates the point with the following example: a patient was given a prescription by his doctor and told, 'Take this'; the patient returned to the doctor having eaten the piece of paper on which the prescription was written—and feeling much better immediately.

Like jailers with their prisoners, some doctors internalise their dysphoric impulses to fester and choke them. Wretched personal and family lives, forever-unrealised goals of contentment and achievement, chronic depression, alcohol and drug abuse... the list of miseries that haunts some is endless, making a stark contrast with their public image as selfless and successful healers. Every doctor knows colleagues who renew philosopher Ralph Waldo Emerson's observation that the majority of men (and women) lead lives of quiet desperation. How many mornings do they look in the mirror and see themselves there?

One explanation may lie in the peculiar intimacy of medical care. Patients put themselves in the care of their doctor and want to believe in the person they have chosen. Being on a pedestal feeds the need of the doctor to be a successful healer, for many it is the raison d'être behind taking up the profession. In an age of equality, patient rights and informed consent, patients can behave any way they like and still expect treatment as a right. Only the doctor can be held to blame; the arbitrariness of life or death is not a matter for the state. The same doctor has to be a combination of priest, counsellor, pharmacologist, horologist, talkshow host and healer—in short, the demiurge of our society.

Doctors look at the postmodern world with fear and loathing. Dissatisfaction with doctors is not new. Ancient writers like Plato complained that physicians insisted on treating slaves with the same care they gave to free men or philosophers— and that they treated sick philosophers like slaves. Chaucer said his doctor believed that gold in his pocket was the best of all treatments. Francis Bacon, reflecting the experiences of many, coined the line 'Cure the disease and kill the patient'.

Now patients beat up doctors if refused drugs to feed their addiction, they sue if not told about the one-in-a-million chance of a complication, and they have doctors deregistered for sleeping with them. An overarching sense of entitlement, a conviction that the world is always to blame when anything goes wrong and a refusal to accept responsibility for their actions make an unpalatable combination for idealistic medical souls whose youthful Zeitgeist was formed by the adventures of television's 'Dr Kildare' and Dr Christiaan Barnard.

In this scenario there is no accommodation for dissident emotions from the healer, or for doctors behaving like patients. How many doctors, if they are truly honest, seeing the same doleful face across the desk or bed yet again have not wished for an early death to relieve them of the burden of dealing with wretched, peevish ingratitude (or clinging adulation)? Take that one step further: in a single, unguarded, impulsive moment, a patient dangling on the business end of a needle, a few air bubbles, an extra squirt of morphine...

Of course the vast majority of doctors do not respond to these murderous impulses, but find other means of coping. The psychiatrist uses huge doses of drugs to sedate patients; the surgeon grudgingly doles out minute amounts of painkillers regardless of discomfort; the petty tyrant considers every patient a shirker and refuses exemption from duty. Black humour is another means, which is why there was such an outcry from the public—and a roar of recognition from doctors—when Samuel Shem's *The House of God* was published: gomer, crumble, cactus, thick-file patient, PPP (piss poor protoplasm), flk (funny looking kid)... just a few examples of the abbreviated etymology used in the gulag of casualty, admissions ward and clinic.

In recognition of the demiurge principle, psychiatrist Humphrey Osmond described the three facets of the medical role as sapiential, authoritarian and charismatic. Sapience, of course, comes from training and experience, while authority is not just implicit, but constantly reiterated by the title: Doctor. The charismatic role accounts for the fact that doctors are dealing with powerful and mysterious forces. As illness and death are not amenable to reason, how or when anyone is ultimately affected is purely random. For that reason, doctors could not be expected to be entirely reasonable; in fact, they are rewarded for being arbitrary.

One of the first to examine the problems of English doctors in general practice was psychoanalyst Michael Balint. The Hungarian-born Balint ran study groups where GP participants in the National Health Service spoke frankly about reactions to their patients. Patients saw many things in their doctors unrelated to the technical process of treatment. Regardless of the complaints the patient brought in to the consultation, the doctor had the power to determine the course of investigation and treatment and, through that, the outcome—prescribing the 'Doctor' as the drug.

Balint concluded that the single most important factor affecting the outcome of treatment in the majority of consultations is the doctor's 'Apostolic Role'. Doctors had the power not only to heal but cause unforeseen, if not lethal, side effects. Doctors, he felt, needed to learn to recognise these reactions, unconscious or otherwise, and decide whether they were shaping the direction of treatment in an inappropriate fashion.

Osmond's triad of the doctor's role is an apt formulation. All doctors include these three factors to a varying degree in their personality; when one factor is overarching, then problems occur. In short, what was intended to be a mutual collaboration and beneficial process of treatment from someone who had a calling to the profession, medicine has become a highly adversarial, consumer-driven interaction.

Modern high-technology medical care ignores that doctors and patients are bound together by a common cause—a fatal flaw. In most cases, this will result in a successful parting when agreed-upon goals are obtained; in some cases, both sink, dragging each other down under the recriminations of failure, misunderstanding, hubris and entitlement. Far from politically correct notions about the doctor–patient relationship, there is nothing new under the sun. They're stuck with each other, exercising an indirect control they do not always understand. The further (higher) they go, the greater the potential for failure. After all, all life ends in death. In the end, doctors and patients are like reluctant Siamese twins; they soar together like Dedalus and Icarus: one flies to the sun, one crashes to the earth. This environment is a potent nidus for the future killer.

5

Early medical murder

It is seldom that such familiarity with the means of death should be shown without long experience.

Lord Campbell, sentencing Dr William Palmer to death in 1856

There has always been medical murder, but the phenomenon was first documented in the nineteenth century, when the perpetrators of this practice increased beyond the occasional trickle to a small but regular stream of offenders. There are several reasons why medical murder began to escalate. Firstly, doctors had access to a range of powerful medications for sedation or analgesia, coupled with a new means of administration: the syringe. Control of drugs was lax to the point of being nonexistent and any doctor would soon learn the lethal effects of such drugs as morphine, arsenic and strychnine. Secondly, doctors were drawing away from their competitors: quacks, herbalists, bonesetters and other alternative practitioners. The movement to institutionalise the profession gathered pace, facilitated by stunning advances such as antisepsis (to avoid post-operation infections) and anaesthesia (to allow patients to be unconscious during operations). The result was not just an exponential increase in status, but in power. And the power of medical practice was a potent attraction to the potential killer, whether they recognised it at the time or not.

The nineteenth-century medical killers were murderers who happened to be doctors and used their skills to this end, tending to kill patients only if they were personally involved with them.

The first doctor ever convicted for using morphine as a murder weapon was Dr Edme Castaing, in early nineteenth-century Paris. Castaing, 27 years old, needed money to maintain an extravagant lifestyle. He was treating Hippolyte Ballet, a wealthy patient dying of tuberculosis. Hippolyte had written a will excluding his feckless brother Auguste. In response, Auguste arranged with Castaing to speed up his brother's demise and destroy the new will, which meant the estate then went to him. At autopsy, it was decided that Hippolyte had died from an unknown poison.

Castaing then decided to kill Auguste to get his money. Incredibly, confirming that most criminals, especially accomplices, are not over-endowed with intelligence, Auguste agreed to make a will in Castaing's favour. Having prudently checked with a lawyer that the will was valid, Castaing took Auguste for a ride to the country and poisoned his wine at a local inn. Auguste was seen by two doctors but died shortly afterwards. At autopsy, it was determined that he had the signs of morphine poisoning, and Castaing was charged with the murders of both Ballet brothers.

At the trial, doctors gave differing opinions on Hippolyte's death. The great Laennec, inventor of the stethoscope, was unsure of the cause of death but could not exclude poisoning. Various experts listed amounts of 10–100 grains of morphine as lethal, when in fact less than one grain can be sufficient to kill the non-habitual user. Aside from contraction of the pupils, the only sign of death by poisoning was the presence of morphine in Auguste's body. The jury found Castaing guilty of murdering Auguste, but not Hippolyte, and he was duly dispatched in the French manner with the assistance of Dr Guillotine's invention.

Across the Channel, Dr William Palmer not only killed at will but found a method to ensure that the deaths subsidised his hedonistic lifestyle. His modus operandi was to take out insurance policies on individuals he knew, many of whom were unaware that he had done this, then terminate them with various poisons and collect the payouts. Palmer's early life indicated a reckless nature, to say the least, involving regular exposure to the effects of various poisons, including alcohol. He was apprenticed to a pharmacist but was sacked after he stole money. Following this, he won an apprenticeship to a local doctor, but it ended in disgrace over sexual impropriety. His studies at the Stafford Infirmary were peremptorily concluded when a plumber died after a brandy-drinking contest. His longsuffering but determined mother then got him into St Bartholomew's Hospital, where he obtained a medical diploma in two years.

Palmer was dedicated to gambling and womanising, despite maintaining a domestic image as a devoted, church-loving husband. He was thought to have fathered at least ten illegitimate children who were later disposed of by poisoning. To cover his trail, Palmer had the assistance of the aged Dr Bamford who was happy to write out medical certificates on the hapless victims for a small gratuity. Here is evidence of another trend: murderous doctors may get assistance from other medical figures who are either dominated by their personality and driven by fear, bribed or too passive to avoid collusion. As his debts reached astronomical heights, he poisoned his father-in-law, a horse-racing companion and finally his wife, the latter two being heavily insured by him. Palmer's earnings from these killings did not last long before he turned on his brother Walter. Before he could collect on this, however, he was arrested for the death of a racehorse owner, John Parsons Cook. No strychnine was found at Cook's autopsy, but Palmer was charged with causing the death of his wife and father-in-law. Antimony was found in the exhumed remains and he was duly found guilty.

Lord Campbell's comments on sentencing Palmer to death summed up the professional advantage doctors had in the murder business: 'It is seldom that such familiarity with the means of death should be shown without long experience.' Hanged at Stafford on 14 June 1856, Palmer was immortalised as a waxwork in the Chamber of Horrors at Madame Tussaud's. His crimes led to a special Act of Parliament, making it illegal to take out an insurance policy on someone's life when their death would cause the insurer financial loss.

After 1880 the scenario changed. While psychopaths have been around as long as doctors, the late nineteenth century saw the rise of the serial killer, a murderer who took a specific interest in the process of death and killing. About the same time as 'Jack the Ripper' came to public notice,[1] two very different doctors were engaging in their own kind of serial murder: Thomas Cream and H.H. Holmes.

Dr Thomas Cream, dubbed the 'Lambeth Poisoner', was the first serial killer to be hanged in Britain. Cream's apprehension resulted from systematic police work and forensic analysis, showing that it was no longer as easy to get away with wanton murder. Thomas Neill Cream, the first of eight children in his family, graduated in medicine at McGill University in 1876. Shortly afterwards he was confronted by an angry, gun-toting mob led by the father of Flora Brooks, a young woman whom Cream had seduced. Flora admitted, while being examined by her family doctor, to having had an abortion performed by Cream. Holding him at gunpoint, Mr Brooks forced Cream to marry Flora. The morning after the wedding, Flora woke up to find that Cream had disengaged himself to London, leaving a note (optimistically) promising to keep in touch.

Cream had further training at St Thomas' Hospital in London, gaining a certificate in midwifery when he could distract himself from carousing with the women of the music halls and taverns. Completing his studies in Edinburgh, Cream set up practice in London, Ontario, in 1878. When a pregnant patient, reeking of chloroform used for an abortion, was found dead, he had to move to Chicago to avoid the investigation. There he continued doing abortions. Several patients died but no action was taken.

In Chicago Cream began marketing an elixir for epilepsy. One of his patients, Daniel Stott, swore by the medication and would send his wife to Cream's office for the pills. Cream had an affair with her, and when Stott eventually became suspicious, Cream added strychnine to Stott's medication. This time the authorities were alerted, Cream was charged and convicted, and sentenced to life in Joliet (Illinois) State Penitentiary.

This, it would be thought, was the end of his medical and murder career. However, using political connections with a bribe arranged by his brother, Cream was able to get out of jail after ten years and return to the scene of old delights in London in 1891. Setting up a practice in Lambeth as Dr Thomas Neill MD, Cream embarked on a spree of poisoning prostitutes with strychnine. His modus operandi was to pick up a prostitute and slip her some pills, suggesting she looked unwell, or that the pills would prevent venereal disease. Cream would then leave while the woman proceeded to die an agonising death by strychnine poisoning. Only one woman— Lou Harvey (aka Louisa Harris)—survived by throwing away the pills.

Cream's arrogance, vanity and boastfulness made him believe he was untouchable; but it was also his downfall as he was eventually arrested. In this regard, he was displaying a characteristic of serial killers, namely a desire to revisit the scene of the crime, enjoy the vicarious pleasure from the shock effect of the killing on others. Before his arrest, Cream befriended Detective John Haynes, foolishly demonstrating to him an uncanny knowledge of the murder cases, including the names of two unknown victims, one of whom was Matilda Clover. Forensic analysis sealed the case; Clover's body was exhumed and found to contain strychnine.

Cream was arrested on 3 June 1892. Maintaining his innocence, Cream remained composed at the trial. It was not until the bailiff brought Lou Harvey to the courtroom that Cream appeared disconcerted. After Harvey gave testimony of her encounter with 'the doctor', Cream was done for. On 21 October 1892, he was found guilty of murdering four women.

Sentenced to death, Cream was hanged on 16 November. His final words as he dropped on the scaffold were 'I am Jack...' fuelling the belief in some minds that he was Jack the Ripper. However, as Cream was in prison while the Ripper was active, not to mention his preference for poisoning as opposed to slashing, it is clear that the two characters were different men.

Across the Atlantic, medical serial murder was given an exponential fillip by Dr Harry Howard Holmes, reported to have killed at least 200 women in his 'murder castle' in Chicago between 1892 and 1896. He was the first serial killer to be hanged in America. Starting off in life with the name of Herman Mudgett, he came from a small New Hampshire town. From an early age he liked dissecting animals. Regarded as highly intelligent, Mudgett finished school and eloped with Clare Lovering. He finished medical school at Ann Arbor six years later.

During this time, Mudgett's behaviour was bizarre and criminal. He avoided lectures, spending his time in the anatomy laboratory dissecting bodies, including mutilating their features. In addition, he would steal corpses, discarding them around the town and collecting insurance policies he had taken out in their names. The policies, presumably, were taken out when they were still meant to be alive. Showing the financial amorality that was such a recurrent feature of his behaviour, he stole from a publisher who employed him as an agent, and used someone else's money that was intended to pay for a barn.

As a physician, Mudgett was a failure and went bankrupt, moving on to a series of down-at-heel jobs, including work in a lunatic asylum. Here he was caught in a scandal when a patient who paid him to assist with an escape was found drowned in a pond. When a customer in Philadelphia died from using a potion he had dispensed, Mudgett fled to Chicago, setting up in the comfortable suburb of Englewood. Having long since disposed of his wife, he arranged that his parents be notified that he was dead. By this time, he needed another alias. The papers were full of stories about the London Ripper, so it may not have been a coincidence that he took the surname of 'The World's Greatest Detective' who had come to public awareness at the same time.[2] The newly christened 'H.H. Holmes' never practised medicine after he moved to Chicago, working instead as a pharmacist. He put his medical knowledge to good use however, using anaesthetics such as chloroform and ether to stupefy victims, in addition to a range of hypnotic drugs and other poisons. Holmes was adept at drawing people into his network, exploiting and then disposing of them when they became a problem or were likely to expose his activities. Like many psychopaths, his manner was extraordinarily glib and convincing, and he seemed to be able to gull women with great ease. Holmes seemed incapable of doing anything honestly if he could cheat, lie or deceive. He constantly engaged in fraudulent schemes, such as a cure for alcoholism and a patent on a machine alleged to turn water into natural gas. He would avoid paying for anything he purchased and, when the police came round to investigate, he was always able to talk his way out of it.

He built an elaborate three-storey 'palace'. The ground floor had his pharmacy, offices, shops and restaurants. His living quarters were on the second floor and the upper floor had his office and several dozen sleeping rooms for guests. The building was carefully designed to his specifications, with blind passages, doors that did not open and hidden chambers. The warren-like set-up led to one place: an elaborate chamber alongside his office in which to imprison, torture and kill his victims. Holmes became addicted to watching his victims' drawn-out deaths. To this end, victims were either lured or deposited in the chamber in a stuporose state. The air was sucked out and the victim killed with poison gas, Holmes watching the whole process through a peep-hole. He would then take the bodies, first raping them, then performing hideous acts of dissection. The bodies were incinerated or, in some cases, boiled down and flensed, the skeletons passed to an associate to be sold to medical schools.

Eventually the game was up, and Holmes set off across the country with the family of an associate, killing off the man's three daughters in the process. He was found guilty of murder and sentenced to be executed. In prison, he wrote a lurid and largely incredible biography for a newspaper, going off to his execution with some equanimity. After his death, the 'palace' was burned to the ground.

One reason Holmes was able to get away with it for so long was the transient nature of life in Chicago. Young women from distant areas would arrive, seeking work as a secretary or shop assistant, their movements after that unknown to anyone close to them. It was a similar situation to that prevailing in Whitechapel where the Ripper operated, and Holmes was later referred to as the 'American Ripper'.

None of the cases described here was strictly speaking the murder of patients; with the exception of Cream and Holmes, they were perpetuated by psychopathic doctors who were able to use medical knowledge to obtain poison to murder people they knew, rather than patients. If it were not to dispose of inconvenient wives or lovers, it was to acquire money, usually due to debts from gambling or an extravagant lifestyle. With the exception of the above two, it is unlikely the killers had any interest in the death of the victim, other than as a means to an end. But they were all doctors, and their modus operandi was an indication of what was to come.

6

A doctor's own story

Dr Harold's Shipman's relentless course of quiet killing

When a doctor goes wrong, he is the first of criminals.
He has nerve and he has knowledge.

Conan Doyle, *The Adventure of the Speckled Band*

In the town of Hyde, Manchester, the darkness comes early on a winter afternoon. In a small apartment a 74-year-old woman hears the doorbell. Wheezing slightly and suppressing a bubbly cough, she walks slowly to the door, opening it without checking. A man of medium height, wearing a padded coat against the cold, walks in carrying a doctor's bag. He has large glasses and a full beard; his lips cannot be seen; his small eyes seem watery, a little unfocused. He nods his head, greeting her in a warm fashion, speaking with a northern accent.

The woman's features brighten immediately. 'Oh Doctor, it's so nice of you to come round to me, I know you've had a busy day what with the flu epidemic and all and wanting to get home to be with your family. Would you like a cup of tea? I've got some cakes still from Tesco.'

The doctor puts his hand reassuringly on her shoulder. 'Thank you, my dear, but I had something before I left the surgery. Why don't we sit down and have a chat before I check you.'

He indicates the comfortable chair in the lounge with a small side table on which sits a half-empty cup of tea. 'Sit there, and I'll get my instruments out. You finish your tea, now.'

The patient puts herself back in the chair, the doctor opens his bag, removing a disposable syringe and needle, a sterilised wipe, a velcro cuff for taking blood and several glass vials marked with brightly coloured writing. On closer inspection of the vial, the words diacetylmorphine can be seen. He tentatively flexes the glass stem of the sealed vial and, with a sudden brisk motion, snaps it off contemptuously and—oddly— tosses it back into the open bag.

While preparing his apparatus, the doctor chats amicably to the patient, asking how her son, a miner who lost his job, is doing and when she is expecting another visit from her daughter and grandson. The patient, well acquainted with the routine, responds with *approval. She knows that he follows rugby football and mentions the local team's recent victory.*

The doctor allows her to chat uninterrupted for several minutes, then he leans forward, his eyebrows slightly raised. 'Why don't you lie back on the chair, I need to give you a shot. It's something new for this bronchitis that's going around. You'll feel right as rain afterwards.'

Her doctor has completed his preparation. The clear viscous fluid has been sucked out of the vial with a slight metallic snort, then drawn back in the syringe and the plunger flexed to expel a few tiny bubbles from the gleaming surgical-steel needle tip which is held upright for a brief moment of inspection.

The patient settles back, her right arm outstretched on the arm of the chair. She is used to the routine, having had blood taken on a number of occasions. The cuff is tied round the thin arm, a mottled blue serpentine vein stands out at the bend of the elbow. The doctor bends over her, breathing slightly as if from some inner tension, and slides the needle expertly into the vein, drawing back the tiny gush of dark-blue blood that puffs into the barrel of the syringe, then sliding the plunger forward in a steady, deft motion.

'This will only take a minute,' he says, flicking the cuff loose on her arm and standing back. The patient looks at Dr Shipman with almost rapturous appreciation as her head lolls back against the armchair.

On 31 January 2000—an ominous harbinger for the new millennium—a bespectacled and visibly fraying doctor faced a jury before a packed courtroom in Preston, Manchester, as they came in to deliver their verdict on a series of charges unprecedented in British justice. Dr Harold Shipman, a 54-year-old general practitioner in solo practice in the nearby town of Hyde, was charged with murdering fifteen patients, aged 49–82 years, with lethal injections of diamorphine (the medical name for heroin) he had stockpiled.

Most of Shipman's victims were elderly women who lived alone, and they regarded Shipman as a trusted friend. They died between 1995 and 1998. On the pretext of taking a blood sample or giving an injection, he injected each of his victims with 30 mg of heroin, a lethal dose. None of the victims had any idea they were being killed. They slipped away into the arms of Morpheus, unaware that the doctor they so trusted was Britain's worst serial killer. Shipman stayed with them as their life ebbed away over the next few minutes, then continued his rounds or returned to his surgery. He would backdate the patients' computer records to create false medical histories to suggest they had died of natural causes.

Shipman's killing spree ended with the death of Kathleen Grundy (82), a former mayoress of Hyde. Police had investigated the doctor six months before his arrest but failed to establish anything further than 'rumour and tittle-tattle'. By the time he killed Mrs Grundy, Shipman was killing one person every ten days and almost 80 per cent of his victims were female. The difference this time was the unexpected appearance in the mail to Mrs Grundy's solicitor of a forged will leaving all her possessions to Shipman. The Grundy will was obviously contrived, if not grossly amateurish. It was Shipman's final gamble. In the remote event that he got away with it, he would have been financially set to leave medical practice and retire—or move somewhere to continue killing; if not, the forgery was likely an announcement to the world of the termination of his murder career.

At the start of the trial, the police were investigating 137 deaths; by May 2000, they had looked into almost 200 deaths. It became clear that Shipman was not a well-meaning doctor who might have overdosed a few terminally ill patients to relieve their suffering, but an unparalleled medical murderer, a serial killer to dwarf all previous contenders. Police said at least 46 patients had been murdered and another 23 charges could follow. Considering the period Shipman had been in practice, the list of victims could stretch back to his internship at Pontefract General Infirmary. Press speculation became increasingly wild, citing first 100 and later 1000 possible murders. What was beyond doubt was that Shipman was Britain's most prolific serial killer, one of the world's worst. What made it more harrowing was that Shipman had been completely free to operate in the houses, rooms and units of anonymous suburbs, a medical Jekyll and Hyde wandering through Little-Old-Lady-Land, unsheathing a lethally loaded syringe, droplets of silent sudden death oozing out of the tip of the velated surgical-steel needle as he killed them off one by one by one.

Shipman's ordinariness permits an unusually fine-grained study of his life. He appeared to lead an unremarkable suburban existence with a wife and four children. There are serial killers who have managed this on occasion, but it is hardly possible to perform such a detailed study on, say, Swango.

Harold Frederick Shipman,[1] always to be known as Fred, was born in Nottingham, United Kingdom, on 14 January 1946, one of thousands of children born in the immediate post-war baby boom. His working-class parents, Harold and Vera Shipman, married in 1937. They were devout Methodists. Harold Shipman senior was a council lorry (truck) driver.

There were large gaps between all the children: Pauline, the eldest, was born in 1938 before her father went away to military service, and Clive followed four years after Fred. This meant that Fred was to some extent raised as an only child in his early years.

It was thought Shipman came from a close and loving home. In fact, there was a serious divide between his parents. Harold Shipman senior was an uncomplicated man who liked a bet. His wife Vera, five years younger, was unreservedly ambitious, having little in common with her husband, pinning all her hopes on Fred, the brightest of the children, and the only one in the family to get to university. Vera kept her children from mixing with the other children in the housing estate. Vera paid Fred special attention; he was always carefully dressed and neat, continuing to wear a bow tie during his years in practice in acknowledgement. And, from an early age, Shipman reciprocated. The closeness between the two was legendary; they were described in the family as being 'like twins'. Fred had a precocious puberty with facial hair at the age of thirteen and would sleep in his mother's bed when his father was away, raising the inevitable although impossible to confirm suspicion of incest.

The teenage Shipman, stocky and muscular, did well at rugby and athletics. He was a good, rather than spectacular, student until his final year in high school, but he was determined to go to medical school from an early age. However, when he was seventeen, Vera got lung cancer. She would spend long hours sitting in a chair in agony, the only relief, as her son noted, was morphine injections from the doctor. At some level, the image of his mother sitting in a chair, struggling against pain and the sigh of relief as the injection was administered, must have been profoundly imprinted on the shattered young man who spent the night she died running through the streets in the rain.

Shipman returned to school after the weekend, telling classmates in a matter-of-fact way of Vera's passing. After his mother's death, Shipman wore an emotional mask and hid his feelings—a characteristic feature of his behaviour all his life. He seemingly put his grief behind him and got on with his life. He used to sniff Sloane's Liniment,[2] an indication of his need for the emotional damping provided by drugs. When his grades plummeted, he repeated the examinations and got into Leeds Medical School in September 1965.

In his first year at medical school, Shipman stayed in a boarding house. He met Primrose Oxtoby on a bus, and he made a rapid impression on her. She had just left school and was trying to break free of her strict parents, so she needed little persuasion to take up with Shipman. For an avowed elitist like Shipman, Primrose was a surprising choice. She was poorly educated, considered unattractive, paid scant attention to appearance and seemed to have little in common with her husband except for complete dedication to her partner. The couple started dating and Primrose fell pregnant within a short time. As was the custom at the time, they married. Primrose's parents were unhappy about the situation from the start and Shipman, with his typical arrogance, antagonised them to such an extent there was no further contact. Shipman's own father wasn't pleased with the marriage, and they became estranged.

Having a young family to support, Shipman was largely un-noticed during his time at medical school. His social ineptitude and innate feelings of superiority made him keep his distance from other students. Living away from home for the first time, still trying to understand his mother's death, with a young wife and baby to support while dealing with the well-known burdens of medical school, he was under more pressure than most. Shipman's reaction to all this—kept well buried—must have been one of confusion, dismay and anger. He started to experiment with morphine. The circumstances in which he obtained it are unknown, but it would not have been too difficult to steal supplies in the wards or emergency department during training. It is reported that his wife found him slumped over in a chair after he injected himself.

Graduating in 1970, Shipman did his internship at Pontefract General Infirmary, followed by an additional two and a half years of paediatrics and obstetrics/gynaecology residency. By the time he completed his residency, Shipman was addicted to pethidine. He later claimed that he used the drug to sleep after working long hours. It was during this time that Shipman probably killed 72-year-old Ruth Highley, the first death certificate he signed. In a significant move, he elected to go into general practice, rather than specialise in hospital. This fuelled his resentment of specialists, widely regarded as high-flyers compared to GPs, always in evidence at meetings when he would make scenes trying to challenge them. Had Shipman gone on to specialise, it is likely his drug dependency would have been detected sooner and his killing career aborted.

In March 1974, Shipman joined the Abraham Ormerod Medical Centre at Todmorden in Yorkshire. He soon made a good impression with his hard work and dedication to patients. He was a heavy prescriber, freely dispensing amphetamines for weight loss to young women, something that would have undoubtedly added to his popularity. This feature of his treatment behaviour, heavy-handedness with drugs, is a consistent feature in dysfunctional and dangerous doctors. During his time at the centre, Shipman signed 22 death certificates, more than double that of anyone else at the practice, but this did not attract any attention.

Shipman started having blackouts and was tested for epilepsy by a physician. As a result, he was not permitted to drive and his wife would take him out to do home visits. Marjorie Walker, the practice receptionist, was tipped off by a local chemist that Shipman was ordering large quantities of pethidine. A senior partner in the centre learned that patients had not received their medication. By this stage, Shipman was injecting pethidine every two hours, ruining the veins in his arms and legs. Confronted by the partners at a meeting, he admitted using up to 700 mg of pethidine a day, claiming he had become addicted from the requirement to try it during medical training—a highly unlikely tale. He said he had been depressed since he started using the drug. The doctors insisted he go to hospital, which he refused. After a six-week stand-off, the matter was investigated by a Health Department official. Shipman could not demur any longer and was admitted to The Retreat, a psychiatric facility in York.

Shipman spent over a year at The Retreat. At a group session, he made a passing (and, in retrospect, chilling) reference to 'killing urges', but immediately laughed it off. Once the worst of the withdrawal from drugs was behind him, he played his patient game with skill, putting on a front of insight, regret and desire to change.

As was the requirement at the time, Shipman was investigated by the police and the General Medical Council (GMC), standing down from the medical register. On 13 February 1976, he pleaded guilty at the Halifax Magistrates Court to three offences of obtaining ten ampoules of 100 mg pethidine by deception, three charges of unlawfully possessing pethidine, and two of forging prescriptions. He asked for a further 74 offences to be taken into consideration. He was given a £600 fine and escaped a jail sentence.

Shipman's marriage was strained but the couple continued to live with their two children, later having two more sons. Before he could apply to return to practice, he was examined by two psychiatrists, convincing them he had put his drug problems behind him. The psychiatrists, one a forensic psychiatrist, concurred, recommending he could return to practice. This was the only time Shipman saw a psychiatrist before he was arrested on murder charges. After his arrest, this caused something of a sensation, but it is difficult to see how the two doctors examining Shipman could have had any inkling that he was any other than one of the many doctors who develop a dependency problem in response to the pressures of medical practice. Furthermore, they were right: there is no evidence that Shipman returned to using drugs.

In less than two years, without having to appear before the GMC's Professional Conduct Committee, Shipman was back in practice. In 1977 he started at the Donnybrook House Group Practice in Hyde, Manchester. Hyde, population 35,000, was a pleasant town of no great distinction that had one source of notoriety. It was in Hattersley, a council estate near Hyde, that Ian Brady and Myra Hindley, the 'Moors Murderers' who committed appalling torture on their child victims, were arrested in 1965.

Shipman's work rate and devotion to elderly patients soon struck a chord, and there was a long waiting list to see him. Shipman was highly regarded. A patient, hearing that she had been accepted onto Shipman's list, said it was 'like winning the lottery'. Paul Spencer, a patient whose signature Shipman later forged on the will of his last victim said, 'I genuinely thought he was a great doctor, very intelligent. I went to see him with different things, and he always had time to talk. You would expect to be kept waiting... but you accepted it because you knew he would spend time with you. There was a year-long wait to get onto his list: he was the most popular doctor in Hyde.'

Shipman's popularity with patients was not always evident to others. His arrogance towards everyone else, even colleagues, was insistent. He mercilessly harassed practice staff and did not hesitate to humiliate them, seeming to home in on a secretary or nurse he disliked until they were forced to leave the practice. There may have been some overtones of defensiveness in this; some staff were married to doctors and his wife was accused of developing the airs of the 'Doctor's Wife'.

His conviction that he was always right about diagnosis or treatment was unshakable. At medical meetings, he hectored specialists or speakers, oblivious that he was out of his depth or making a fool of himself.

A control freak of Olympic proportions, Shipman was a tyrant who made dictatorial demands on his family, barking down the phone that they sit at the table but not eat dinner until he got home, sometimes as late as 10 p.m. Friends observed his insensitivity to his children, pushing them excessively to study. His eldest daughter Sarah eventually moved out of home to escape his constant bullying.

In February 1985 Shipman's father died, leaving Fred junior out of the will, symbolising his ostracism from the family. Fred senior had been estranged since the marriage to Primrose and father and son had not been in contact for a year. Shipman was devastated by the death. Comments were made that he seemed even more isolated. He drank more, unusually getting drunk at cocktail parties he attended with his wife. He started collecting trophies, items like jewellery, from patients he killed—a common practice of serial killers—storing the items in a box; possibly he saw this as a substitute for not receiving anything in his father's will.

A complaint made in August 1985 that Shipman had breached confidence about a patient who died was not investigated. In 1989 Shipman was sued by a patient for causing him to overdose on his anti-epilepsy medication. He admitted his error, and the matter was settled without further investigation by the GMC. In February 1992, he was fined by the local medical service committee after a complaint that he failed to visit a patient who had a stroke. Again, this was seen as an isolated event and no further investigation was conducted.

Increasingly aware of the risks of detection, Shipman needed complete control of his practice to avoid answering to anyone. The only way to do this was to work on his own. In late 1991, Shipman left the Donnybrook House Group Practice without notice, taking with him his patient list, several receptionists and the nurse. In addition, he refused to pay tax and demanded to be paid out for his share of the building. Shipman's behaviour was self-serving, inconsiderate and unprofessional but it was pointless for the practice to sue him. If nothing else, it was a graphic example of his sheer mendacity.

Shipman established his solo practice, The Surgery, at 21 Market Street in July 1992; he was finally in control of the killing factory. Over 3000 patients were registered, a large number for a single doctor. Such was the esteem in which he was held that a Shipman's Patient Fund raised money to buy equipment for the surgery. Later some of these patients, unable to believe that their doctor could be a murderer, set up a support group. Practice audits showed that he was one of the five top drug prescribers in the area and would go to some lengths to treat a patient, rather than refer them to a hospital when needed. In 1994, he was found to be prescribing excessive amounts of benzodiazepines but, in view of his good record, no steps were taken.

Shipman's killings escalated over the next six years until the high death rate of his patients began to attract attention and he was arrested. That there was a high death rate among his patients was laughed off by his colleagues and the public, attributed to the fact that he treated so many elderly people who were ill and likely to die. Receptionists at the Hyde group practice nicknamed Shipman 'Dr Death', always a good, if empirical, indicator of a disproportionate death rate.

In retrospect, Shipman's frantic workrate and attention to patients was to maintain the assembly-line process to feed his addiction to killing. He had to be able to go on house calls when it was least likely that anyone else was around, or that the coincidence of the deaths would be noted by anyone not under his thrall at the practice. Furthermore, he needed to rummage through the dead person's belongings for their supply of narcotics to use on the next victim. On some occasions, he killed patients when someone was next door, unable to control himself and becoming over-confident.

John Shaw, the taxi driver who transported many of the elderly women who saw Shipman, became suspicious, as did Alan Massey who operated the funeral home that buried many of the patients. Staff at the funeral home became aware that there was a high percentage of elderly women, invariably found at their home sitting fully dressed in a chair. Massey confronted Shipman about his concerns in 1997, but was reassured by his easy response that all the deaths were appropriately noted in the death certificate book.

In 1998 Dr Linda Reynolds, who worked at the surgery opposite Shipman, was unable to overlook the unusually high death rates of his patients. Doctors had informal agreements to sign the death certificates for each other's deceased patients who were to be cremated. This was regarded as a harmless arrangement to save bureaucratic delays for the doctor and minimise distress for the family. Dr Reynolds's concerns prompted her to contact the South Manchester coroner. The police were requested to investigate the matter, finding the records did not show anything untoward, unaware that Shipman was altering his notes to produce this impression. He was not interviewed and, despite some reservations, the investigations were suspended. The police had failed to check Shipman's criminal record which would have revealed his 1976 conviction for fraudulently obtaining pethidine.

The first inkling that Shipman had committed a very serious crime came after Mrs Grundy's death on 24 June 1998. Kathleen Grundy lived at 79 Joel Lane, an attractive road with terraced houses. Despite her age, Mrs Grundy was healthy and energetic, with little record of illness. She led an active life with friends and family, loved walking and doted on her grandsons. She was renowned for her enthusiasm, kindness and charm.

Two weeks before her death, Shipman asked Mrs Grundy to participate in a survey on aging that required a blood sample and a signature on a consent form. He later traced the signature on to her will. The poorly typed will had been witnessed by two of his patients, but they had not seen anything except a folded-over piece of paper Shipman asked them to sign.

On 23 June 1998, the day of her death, Mrs Grundy told a friend that Shipman was coming to her house the next day to take a blood specimen. The next day Mrs Grundy failed to turn up at a local charity venue at which she usually served lunches, and concerned colleagues paid her a visit. On arrival, they found her home unlocked and Mrs Grundy, fully clothed, curled up dead on the sofa. Shipman, called to examine her, tersely snapped that she'd had a cardiac arrest. He telephoned the coroner's office and wrote a death certificate listing 'old age' as the cause.

On the day Kathleen Grundy died, Hyde solicitors Hamilton Ward had received a typewritten letter, dated two days earlier, stating that Kathleen Grundy wished to leave her entire estate to Dr Harold Shipman. Four days later, they received another letter from an F., J. or S. Smith, claiming to have typed out the will. Twelve days after her death, her only daughter, solicitor Angela Woodruff, received a letter from Hamilton Ward, telling her that they had her mother's will.

Angela Woodruff, who had an earlier copy of her mother's will in her possession, was immediately suspicious, knowing her mother would never disinherit her family, let alone go about things in such a secretive or peremptory fashion. She was certain her mother had never dealt with the solicitors.

Angela Woodruff made inquiries and reported the matter to the police. It soon became clear that the will was a crude forgery, prompting the police to make further inquiries. F/J/S. Smith never came forward as he had never existed.

The police obtained a warrant to search Shipman's surgery and home. He was locking up the rooms after the Saturday morning clinic when they arrived, showing no signs of concern, only his usual arrogance when dealing with officialdom. Asked about a typewriter, he promptly brought a portable Brother typewriter out of the cupboard—it had misaligned E, A and W keys, which was shown to perfectly match the type on the will and the Smith letter.

The Shipman home was in Roe Cross Green in Mottram, several miles from Hyde. When the police entered, they were shocked by the mess: piles of newspapers, gunk on the carpet that stuck to the shoes, and piles of mouldy dishes stacked in the sink. One of the officers later commented that it was the sort of home where you wiped your feet on the way out, not in. It seemed an inappropriate, if not bizarre, setting for a middle-class doctor and his family. The police found containers of medical records, several ampoules of heroin and a large box of oddly assorted jewellery.

Kathleen Grundy's body was exhumed, and the autopsy showed that a lethal concentration of morphine had been administered within three hours of death. Now the police knew they were dealing with a murder. The investigation continued and more bodies of Shipman patients who died between 1995 and 1998 were exhumed for examination. Of fifteen deaths forming the indictment, nine were exhumed, given autopsies and toxicological analysis. The other six bodies had been cremated. The interval between death and autopsy ranged from 38 to 852 days.

Samples for toxicology were limited; anterior thigh skeletal muscle as well as the liver tissue, where available, were analysed for morphine content. As opiates such as morphine accumulate in the hair, samples were analysed in eight cases (including Kathleen Grundy), showing only minute amounts of morphine from post-mortem contamination, thereby scotching Shipman's defence claim at the trial that the patients had been abusing opiates for long periods before they died.

The police soon realised their worst fears: they were dealing with a serial murderer of extraordinary capacity.

Interviewed by the police, Shipman denied all charges, putting on a front of being cooperative and wanting to assist.

However, it quickly became apparent that he was not going to disclose any information, claiming his patients had died of serious illnesses with manifestations which could not be understood by lay people or, as in the case of Kathleen Grundy, that they were abusing drugs.

Shipman, a technology enthusiast, had the latest computer system, keeping all his patient records on one machine in his practice. In October 1996, he updated the Medi-Doc software program. Unbeknownst to him, the new version had a back-up program recording the date and time of each entry. John Ashley, head of the Greater Manchester Police Computer Forensic Unit, examined Shipman's computer records. He would make some entries in the mornings, then more after 4 p.m. The computer backup showed he had backdated entries on the day of Kathleen Grundy's death trying to implicate her as a drug addict. Here was clear proof Shipman had premeditated the killing but was trying to cover his tracks. As it turned out, he did this for a number of other murders.

Statistical analysis revealed a consistent pattern in the fifteen deaths: all were older women; Shipman was present at the death or shortly before; the death would occur suddenly at home and, in fourteen of the fifteen cases, in the afternoon; the correlation between the clinical history and certified cause of death was very weak. Mrs Grundy's death bore all the hallmarks of a Shipman murder. It was an unexpected death in an otherwise healthy elderly woman, occurring soon after a home visit and the administration of diamorphine; friends or relatives of the deceased noted that the front door was unlocked and on arrival, Shipman behaved in an abrupt peculiar manner.

On 7 September 1998 Shipman was charged with fifteen murders and forgery of the Grundy will. Bail was refused and he was put in remand at Strangeways Prison, Manchester. He was soon moved to Preston Prison due to fears for his safety. Later he was taken to Walton Jail in Liverpool before returning to Preston.

On 5 October 1998, Detective Sergeant Mark Wareing and Detective Constable Marie Snitynski questioned Shipman over the death of Winifred Mellor. He had falsified her medical records to show she had a history of heart trouble but the post-mortem showed a fatal level of morphine. An excerpt from the transcript is highly revealing of Shipman's response to being challenged by police officers whom he clearly considered to be his inferiors. The officer questioning Shipman described him as an arrogant individual who wanted to control and dominate the interview, belittling the police and seeing it as a sort of mental game:

DC Marie Snitynski: A home office pathologist, Dr Rutherford carried out that post-mortem examination (on the body of Mrs Mellor)... his findings do not support that this lady died of a coronary thrombosis as you've diagnosed. Would you like to comment on that, that finding?

Harold Shipman: Doctors don't always diagnose a heart attack as a heart attack, they'll call it coronary thrombosis or myocardial ischemia, myocardial infarction to the average run of the mill GP. They are all the same, the patient's dead. With a coronary thrombosis you would expect there would be a bit of heart muscle damaged but you can't [*sic*] have just an electrical disorganisation of the heart which kills you just as effectively and leaves no symptoms at all. No signs sorry. (No) Signs at all.

DC Marie Snitynski: Well in his expert opinion there was nothing to support your diagnosis is what I'm saying.

Harold Shipman: But he couldn't rule out a disorganised electric, electrical activity of the heart.

DC Marie Snitynski: ... Samples (were) taken from Mrs Mellor and there's certainly a high level of morphine still contained in her body. A fatal level to be precise. Can you account for that?

Harold Shipman: No.

DC Marie Snitynski: Well I've got to put it to you doctor that you are the person who administered that lady with the drug, aren't you?

Harold Shipman: No.

DC Marie Snitynski: The levels were such that this woman actually died from toxicity of morphine, not as you wrongly diagnosed. In plain speaking you murdered her... One feature of these statements from the family was that they couldn't believe their own mother had chest pains, angina and hadn't been informed.

Harold Shipman: By, by whom?

DC Marie Snitynski: By her.

Harold Shipman: By her, thank you.

DC Marie Snitynski: They also found it hard to believe that she would refuse any treatment she was given in relation to this diagnosis and I think now that we can answer why that was. Because she didn't have a history of chest complaints and heart disease and angina, did she doctor?

Harold Shipman: If it's written on the records then she had the history and therefore. . .

DC Marie Snitynski: The simple truth is you've fabricated a history to cover what you've done, you'd murdered her and you make up a history of angina and chest pains so you could issue a death certificate and placate this poor woman's family didn't you?

Harold Shipman: No.

DC Marie Snitynski: We've got a statement from a Detective Sergeant John Ashley who works in the field of computers. He has made a thorough examination of your computer, doctor, and the medical records contained on it... A copy of the records as they stand on the computer, but because this man's an expert he's able to interrogate computers and he has gone into this computer in some depth and what he's found is that there are a number of entries that have been incorrectly placed on this record to falsely mislead and to indicate this woman had a history of angina and chest pains. What have you got to say about that doctor?

Harold Shipman: Nothing.

'Nothing' indeed was the response from a doctor whose view was that regardless of the cause 'the patient's dead' and, regardless of his disdain, the likelihood of being discovered was fast becoming a reality.

The police returned to question Shipman, this time in the presence of his lawyer. When told that his alteration of the computer records had been exposed, he collapsed, sobbing on the floor. Shipman never spoke to the police again.

The news of Shipman's arrest spread like wildfire through the town and beyond, causing shock and consternation. Family, patients and friends refused to believe that the doctor they had so trusted, even loved, could be charged with murder. The walls of his rooms were covered with Good Luck cards from patients. His wife Primrose, steadfast in her conviction of her husband's innocence, had no difficulty persuading several colleagues and friends to cough up large sums for his bail, which nevertheless was refused. Jane Ashton-Hibbert wanted to send him a card, and her husband planned to leave his own doctor in favour of Shipman when he was released. It was later found that Ashton-Hibbert's grandmother was probably killed by Shipman and she subsequently set up a support group for families of his patients.

Shipman became deeply depressed after he was arrested, and was put on high doses of medications. Yet he did not lose confidence that he would be exculpated. As well as messages of support from patients and colleagues, he maintained a spirited correspondence with friends and supporters from jail, spiced with cynical commentary on his surroundings, the media feeding frenzy and the steady build-up of the prosecution case against him. He explained the acronyms used in his medical case notes to a correspondent: BANT stood for Big Arse, Nice Tits; FTBI was Failed to Put Brain In; BIBD was Brains in Big Dick. These abbreviations, stock-in-trade examples of medical black humour used to cope with the pressures of clinical work, now seemed worse than cynical: they were ominous, if not sadistic.

In the tradition of doctor prisoners, Shipman—known to all as 'The Doctor'—ran an informal clinic, providing consultation to prisoners and guards who, in turn, regarded his skills highly. He did not, of course, have access to drugs. He also gave advice to prisoners on medical evidence that was used in their trials. To other prisoners Shipman explained that if he had wanted to kill his patients, there were many ways to inject heroin without being discovered: another example of a self-belief that refused to be contradicted by reality. 'My work was faultless. I provided the ultimate care,' he told prisoner Derrick Ismiel. 'I prided myself on my experience in caring for people who were terminally ill. How dare they question my professionalism? People knew me by my work. How can they accuse me of this?'

Starting in October 1999, Shipman's trial was a sensation. It was held at Preston Court, known as the 'Old Bailey of the North', which previously attracted attention with the trial of the two schoolboys who murdered two-year-old Jamie Bulger. The international media flocked to the trial, creating headlines around the world. Previously few UK doctors had been found guilty of murder; Dr Buck Ruxton was one, and only Dr Edward Pritchard both killed and completed death certificates on his wife and mother-in-law. Those with long memories recalled the unsuccessful trial of Eastbourne doctor John Bodkin Adams in 1957.

By the time he came to trial, Shipman had lost over 28 pounds, looking aged and dejected. His face hidden behind a full beard and goggle-like glasses, Shipman seemed an unlikely, if not innocuous, figure to be accused of such heinous crimes. The media always used the same photograph; in it he seemed wooden, closed-off, pensive.

Primrose and their four children attended every day of the trial. Primrose Shipman's behaviour at the trial seemed incongruous; during breaks she handed out sweets from her bag to her children as if attending a concert. The media made unkind comments about her unfashionable dress and hat. But her devotion to her husband was unstinting and there was no doubt that her conviction of his innocence was unswerving.

The fifteen women Shipman was charged with murdering were Maria West, Irene Turner, Lizzie Adams, Jean Lilley, Ivy Lomas, Muriel Grimshaw, Marie Quinn, Kathleen Wagstaff, Bianka Pomfret, Norah Nuttall, Pamela Hillier, Joan Melia, Maureen Ward, Winifred Mellor and Kathleen Grundy.

In his opening address, Prosecutor Richard Henriques QC said police investigations had uncovered a horrific tale of a doctor who developed 'a taste for the drama of taking life' and could be England's most prolific serial killer this century. 'He enjoyed killing these women,' said Henriques. 'He was exercising the ultimate power of controlling life and death.' Before the trial, Shipman's explanation was that all the victims had died from drug overdoses or old age. 'You have a major drugs problem in Hyde amongst the elderly,' he told the incredulous police. If this explanation were to be uncritically accepted, the jury would have to envisage 82-year-old former mayoress Kathleen Grundy driving in her Mini to pick up supplies from her drug dealer. Forensic testing of hair samples from the victims revealed that none had a history of drug abuse.

The prosecution's case revealed just how thin was the screen of deception Shipman erected to cover his trail. He altered the records in six cases to create a false medical history to explain their deaths. In a further six cases, he justified his presence in their homes on the basis of receiving a telephone call beforehand. The records showed that no such calls had been made. Shipman accumulated the lethal narcotics by taking diamorphine vials from the homes of those who died, prescribing it for patients who were well and did not require it or, in several cases, for someone already dead. Pharmacy records easily revealed the discrepancy. The police estimated Shipman had obtained 20,000 mg of morphine between 1993 and his arrest in 1998. It caused a stir when it was revealed that Shipman was convicted in 1976 for obtaining pethidine in much the same way for an addiction, prescribing it for patients and keeping some or all of the drug for himself.

Angela Woodruff took the stand and spoke of her mother as a picture of health: 'We would walk five miles and come in and she would say "Where's the ironing?" We used to joke she was fitter than we were.'

Pathologist Dr John Rutherford described the post-mortems on the nine exhumed victims. None of them had died from old age or natural causes. Rutherford was adamant that the cause of death in each case was morphine toxicity.

The next witness, District Nurse Marion Gilchrist, wept as she recounted what Shipman had told her as Mrs Grundy was exhumed: 'The only thing I did wrong was not have her cremated. If I had her cremated I wouldn't be having all this trouble.' Relatives and friends of the victims revealed Shipman to be a callous and deceitful man who was a compulsive liar.

Shipman did not have a good trial. At the start, he appeared calm, confident, even cocky, taking profuse notes during the prosecution evidence. He made a poor impression, showing no remorse or sympathy towards his victims, on occasions even responding sarcastically to his own counsel's questions.

The sheer implausibility of his claims was most vividly revealed during questioning on the death of Ivy Lomas, perhaps some belated justice considering his attitude to her. Mrs Lomas was a regular patient whom he considered a nuisance. Questioned by the police about her death, he dismissively offered to put up a memorial plaque over her chair in the waiting room. Shipman alleged that Mrs Lomas had taken the morphine in his consulting room where she died. The computer records showed she had been in the room for twenty minutes. It was estimated it would have taken her five minutes to die, during which time he was present.

Under relentless cross-examination by Henriques, Shipman could only offer blanket denials to every charge, his self-assurance wilting each time he responded. The court transcript reveals the dramatic forensic moment when it was clear Shipman's thin house of cards had not only fallen over, but been irretrievably scattered before the wind of prosecutorial accusation.

Q: Dr Shipman, did you see Ivy Lomas take any drug when she was in your consulting room?

A: No Sir, I did not.

Q: If a patient were to administer drugs to herself during an examination would you observe that?

A: Yes of course I would.

Q: If Ivy Lomas herself did not administer the drugs that leaves but one candidate does it not?

In Mr Henriques's words, a 'very long silence' followed. The prosecutor said nothing, leaving the impact to sink in on the jury, the judge, the public and Shipman himself. There was clearly only one candidate, and he was in the witness box.

Shipman's defence alleged the prosecution's case was based solely on 'unreliable and unsafe' toxicological evidence gathered after the bodies of nine women were exhumed and traces of diamorphine found in each of them.

Shipman's barrister, Nicola Davies, attempted to undermine the forensic evidence but it was impossible to make any inroads into the mountain of proof. She sought to have the trial halted because of 'inaccurate and misleading' press coverage. She sought to have the case of Mrs Grundy severed from the other murders because it, alone, had an obvious motive. She sought to persuade the judge to exclude from the jury evidence that Shipman had stockpiled morphine, often by prescribing it in the name of patients who were already dead. She sought to portray Shipman as a kind and caring family doctor. She failed on every count.

Shipman was virtually the only witness for the defence. During testimony he collapsed several times, a mere shell of himself, at times looking to the jury with a pleading expression as if to capture their sympathy. By the time he stepped down from the witness box, Shipman was a broken man.

The jury deliberated for six days, leading to fears they were unable to reach a verdict. When they came back into the court it was impossible to tell what they had decided. It took the jury foreman six minutes to deliver the verdicts in a level tone: guilty of all charges. Shipman was guilty of murdering fifteen patients and forging the will of Kathleen Grundy. Wearing the same light-brown suit and striped tie he had worn throughout the trial, Shipman showed no emotion.

Justice Thayne Forbes told Shipman: 'Finally you have been brought to justice for your wicked, wicked crimes. You abused the trust of these victims—you were, after all, their doctor. You used a calculating and cold-blooded perversion of your medical skills. You have shown no remorse. In your case life must mean life. You must spend the remainder of your days in prison.'

In an unusual move, removing the wig that symbolised judicial authority and anonymity, Justice Forbes turned to the victims' relatives and told them how he admired their 'courage and quiet dignity'.

As the judgment was delivered, a mobile phone went off in Primrose Shipman's handbag. She gave an audible sigh and was comforted by her children. None of the family, who had maintained public silence throughout the trial, would comment to the press, except to tell them that Primrose would stand by her husband.

Following Shipman's conviction, there was a predictable uproar. The victims' families demanded answers, the public asked how they could be protected against murderous doctors and the British Medical Association went into crisis mode when it was revealed that Shipman had been convicted of drug offences in 1976 and been allowed to return to practice without the police or the public being informed. In the wake of Shipman's conviction, one of the first rules to change was the unsupervised arrangement for doctors to sign cremation certificates without having to check the cause of death.

Shipman went to prison professing his innocence, pursuing appeals against the conviction on the grounds of a prejudiced trial due to media publicity; all appeals failed. As a rather irrelevant coda, he was removed from the medical register. As he was to be in jail for the rest of his life, it was decided that the interests of justice would not be served by further trials and the remaining cases against him were closed.

A Department of Health review compared Shipman's clinical notes on patients who had died between 1974 and 1998 with those who had died while registered with similar local practices. Death certificates show that he recorded 297 more deaths than did doctors with comparable practices. The review concluded that the number of excess deaths in Shipman's practice was 236. Although Shipman's peers were present at fewer than 1 per cent of their patients' deaths, Shipman attended 20 per cent and when he wasn't present he frequently had seen his patients shortly beforehand. Relatives and carers were less likely to have been present (40.1 per cent versus 80.0 per cent) at the deaths of Shipman's patients than at deaths in similar practices. Shipman's deaths peaked between 1 p.m. and 6 p.m.; 12 per cent died around 2 p.m. when he usually did home visits versus 2 per cent in similar practices. The proportion of Shipman's patients who died less than 30 minutes after his arrival was nearly three times that of similar practices.

The government announced an inquiry headed by Dame Janet Smith to look into the case and make recommendations. Shipman, continuing to deny his guilt, refused to cooperate and Dame Janet Smith accepted that it was pointless to attempt to question or interview him. Primrose Shipman did not have this prerogative. Shepherded by her son to and from the court, she gave evidence at the inquiry. On at least two occasions, she had given her husband a lift to visit patients who subsequently died at their homes. She was also present, working as the receptionist, when a patient died in the surgery. After the investigation ended, she unsuccessfully appealed for the return of jewellery which had been removed from her home as evidence. Her response to all questions would be described as typical of a hostile witness: 'I don't know' or 'I don't remember'.

The Smith report, 'The Shipman Inquiry', was published in 2001. It concluded that Shipman had unlawfully killed 215 patients, and a real suspicion remained over 45 others. It looked as if he had murdered 260 patients, although other estimates brought the figure closer to 450. This made Shipman far and away one of the world's worst serial killers, and certainly the most prolific medical serial killer in history.

The gradual increase in the pace of killing after 1994 demonstrated an 'addiction' to killing, the report suggests.

Shipman had a compulsion to search for a victim at the earliest available opportunity.

Shipman's choice of victims provided further insight into his thinking. He was particularly prone to kill the terminally ill, the bereaved and patients who were very demanding of his time and resources, whom he regarded as a nuisance or who annoyed him. After his murders, as the relatives assembled, he enjoyed being the omniscient, controlling 'master of ceremonies'. He would give instructions about the removal of the body... give his explanation for death, adding such remarks as 'she was riddled with cancer', said the report. On 7 June 1996, Leah Fogg's daughter asked Shipman to see her mother about bereavement counselling. He did, within three days, and killed Mrs Fogg.

Shipman feared capture, and periodically stopped killing. The analysis of these periods suggested that near-misses may have been the cause. There were no deaths between November 1979 and April 1981, for instance, because Shipman failed in his attempt to kill Alice Gorton. He thought she was dead and was telling her daughter that it would not be necessary to have a post-mortem examination when Mrs Gorton suddenly groaned. She was still alive.

The unexpected arrival of a district nurse during a murder had the same effect in 1989. When he began killing again, he was more likely to go for the terminally ill—in Dame Janet's words, '...as if he were entering the pool at the shallow end to see if he could still kill'.

Shipman was not especially clever. Many of his behaviours and explanations were inept and stereotypical, and were perpetuated by flaws in a broken medical regulatory system; he was caught as soon as he strayed outside the medical domain into a legal one, involving the scrutiny of a will.

Four leading psychiatrists were consulted, but had to make their case at a distance as Shipman refused to attend or co-operate with examinations. The psychiatrists told the inquiry that Shipman's arrogance and over-confidence were 'almost certainly a mask for poor self-esteem'. Addicted to pethidine early in his career, Shipman was 'probably angry, deeply unhappy and chronically depressed' for most of his adult life, they deduced. A person who has one addiction is likely to suffer other forms of addiction. The psychiatrists considered the possibility that Shipman 'might have developed a fear of death and a need to control death'. He may have had a morbid interest in death, experienced a 'buzz of pleasure' from it and felt that death relieved him from 'intolerable pressure or anxiety'. His early victims were terminally ill people who presented the least danger of detection and probably seemed to him to be 'the least morally culpable'. He killed them because they would not threaten his own security and their deaths could perhaps be justified to him in some way.

With the crudely forged will for Kathleen Grundy, his last victim, Shipman would have known her daughter was a solicitor and 'must have been raising a flag to draw attention to what he had been doing', the report said.

'I think it likely that the conflict between what drove him to kill and his fear of detection... must have driven him to the edge of breakdown,' Dame Janet concluded.

After sentencing, Shipman's depression worsened and he was put on suicide watch. However, he settled and seemed to adapt to prison life. Shipman—Prisoner CJ8199—was a model prisoner. Many psychopaths and serial killers find prison a perfectly controlled environment; the limits on behaviour they cannot provide internally are physically imposed, and there is a built-in hierarchy they can easily traduce to their convenience without the messiness and constraints of ordinary society.

He threw himself into study courses and participated in prison activities. According to the inverted hierarchy that operates in jails, as a murderer he was a figure of some status. On one occasion, he rescued a prisoner who attempted suicide in his cell, resuscitating him. With what can only be described as extraordinary irony, considering his plans for himself, he said that life was too valuable to waste.

Visits from Primrose became the central focus for Shipman in prison. His children, as much victims as anyone else in the saga, dropped away and tried to avoid the constant media attention. His eldest daughter Sarah, by then married, was estranged. The others remained supportive of their mother and were reported to be having difficulty accepting what had happened.

On 13 January 2004, after four years of incarceration, Shipman hanged himself in his cell in HMP Wakefield. In keeping with the tabloid spirit, *The Sun* newspaper announced Shipman's suicide with the headline 'Ship Ship Hooray', with a graphic showing how Shipman killed himself. Victims' relatives expressed outrage that he had escaped punishment, and prison authorities, as they always do, expressed stunned amazement that a suicide could occur under their jurisdiction.

Primrose was the sole beneficiary of his will, receiving £24,000 from the NHS widow's pension. The police would not allow her to bury her husband because of the risk of desecration. Due to her reluctance to have him cremated, Shipman's body remained in the morgue for over a year before he was finally cremated in a secret ceremony on 19 March 2005.

The coroner found he had chosen the timing shortly before he turned 60 to ensure that Primrose would be eligible for his

NHS pension. This may have been the finding that Shipman intended, but there must have been more to it. Shipman's prison suicide was as certain as anything could be. Unable to admit that he had in any way been culpable, the act of remaining in prison was a statement to the world of his guilt. Furthermore, as someone whose raison d'être was driven by the power of death, he would have been as obsessed with his own demise as that of his patients.

Shipman had one of the biggest patient lists in the area but ensured that he kept up with practice requirements. He received regular approval from the auditors that he was meeting required practice standards:

> This practice displays an enthusiasm for audit and quality deliverance of care. Audit has become a meaningful integrated part of general practice.

And:

> Great to see a single-handed enthusiastic GP with a rolling programme of audit—keep up the good work!

The second quote is dated January 1998, just nine months before Shipman's arrest.

During Shipman's trial, the judge had told the jury that a guilty verdict did not require a motive. After Shipman was found guilty, one question remained unanswered: why had a doctor, sworn by the Hippocratic Oath to protect and preserve life, alleviate suffering and *primum non nocere* (first do no harm), gone to such appalling extremes, killing his patients in droves?

7

Searching for Shipman

Shipman's serial killing: making sense of the senseless

Everything points to the fact that a doctor with the sinister and macabre motivation of Harold Shipman is a once in a lifetime occurrence.

Professor Liam Donaldson,
Clinical Audit on Dr Shipman

Considering the extent of his clinicides, Shipman is in a league of his own. For the forensic psychiatrist and historian, the first problem is categorising his crimes. Who was this man who perverted his medical role to become killer, rather than healer? What drove a polite and apparently caring general practitioner, leading a comfortable middle-class existence with a wife and four children, to ruthlessly dispatch his patients in such an arbitrary fashion?

From the evidence in the public record, Shipman seemed elusive, above motive, so to speak. Sex did not play any evident part; money—except for the forgery of the Grundy will—was not involved. Excitement at killing, control over death and the uncontrolled use of power were among the suggested motives, but they do not explain much.

Shipman had a single interview with a forensic psychiatrist. Before the trial Dr Richard Badcock examined Shipman to assess if he was fit to be interviewed during police questioning after his arrest in September 1998. Shipman commenced by dealing with him as he had dealt with the police, the lawyers and other investigators—by playing mind games, ducking and weaving questions, and constantly maintaining his absolute denial of any wrong-doing. By the end of the interview, the psychiatrist and GP were at loggerheads. Shipman refused to cooperate again with police and was not examined by other psychiatrists.

The psychiatrist described it as a classic case of necrophilia. Shipman relished his power to terminate life, displaying a sadistic indifference to his victims. Shipman had 'a sense of overwhelming mastery', an obsessive need to control every aspect of his life, both at home and at work. He enjoyed watching his victims die 'at rest and grateful'. The killings gave him 'a sense of relief from tension, oppression, a sense of relief from personal stress'.

One feature of Shipman's personality that was immediately evident to everyone who dealt with him was his overweening arrogance. He regarded almost everyone as his inferior. This sense of superiority, Nietzchean in its manifestation, made him believe he could kill without detection and, later, succeed at his trial. Although he could be sociable, even charming at times, it was frequently observed that he seldom let down his guard, never got close to anyone and was essentially a loner. This is a regular feature of serial killers.

The relationship with his wife Primrose was grossly mismatched. He lost interest in her after she had the children and would sneak off to prostitutes. Their house was a pigsty, a paradoxical situation for a control freak. Primrose Shipman, completely under his thrall, worshipped him to an extreme and refused to accept that he had been guilty of anything. Or did she? After Shipman's death, Primrose refused to relinquish the large box of trinkets, jewellery and other personal effects that Shipman souvenired from his victims (and the authorities had to force her to hand it over). The extent to which she was juggling in her mind the unthinkable is likely to remain an enduring mystery.

Shipman's recreational pursuits were quite wide. He detested dogs and loved cats, a preference that requires no further explanation. He was involved in a project to save the local canal. He would attend school events with his children, was a school governor and frequently watched his son playing rugby. He liked planning and going on European holidays. He relished medical technology and was inordinately interested in computers. This is noteworthy as computers and syringes seem to have had a mordant fascination for him as the indispensable paraphernalia of his murder sprees. After a killing, he would return to the computer and alter the records to hide his path. Yet he made the most simple of errors, unaware that the computer drive would reveal all deletions and therefore expose his alterations.

Serial killers are often interested, if not obsessed, by other murderers, studying them intensely and using them as models.

Shipman, whose intellectual interests were anodyne at best, was reportedly enthralled by a book about the killing career of his colleague Dr William Palmer in the mid-1800s. Palmer killed a number of people, as well as his wife, by poisoning them with his prescriptions, then wrote out their death certificates. Sinificantly, Palmer forged the will of his last victim, trying to obtain his wealth. He was executed by hanging. The analogies between poisoning patients, forging a will to announce the end of the clinicides and finally, death by hanging seem uncannily close. Shipman also watched a television documentary on the career of Dr John Bodkin Adams, suspected of killing 132 patients (see Chapter 8) but, unlike Shipman, getting away with it.

While Shipman was regarded as unstinting in the care of his patients, there was more to it. He was acutely aware of his status as a doctor and always let people know. He was often cynical, brusque, dismissive or unsympathetic to patients yet managed to placate and entice most of them. The frenetic consulting was a process of constant preparation for the clinicides, familiarising himself with the killing ground and meticulously preparing for the moment when he could catch patients alone, swiftly kill them and loot the place for their stock of narcotics, either for his own use or for use on the next victim.

Shipman ruthlessly overawed and manipulated vulnerable friends and relatives at pivotal moments in their lives. As Sam Slater, who lost both his father and sister at Shipman's hands, put it: 'Grief knocks the logic out of you. You are not Sherlock Holmes with a loved one dead. You are just numb, and that's what Shipman played on with all his victims.'

Shipman followed the typical serial killer path of behavioural try-outs and trial runs. An early attempt to kill a younger and more resilient woman led to near-detection; furthermore, she survived in a vegetative state for three months. He refined the technique: elderly women were the easiest, most trusting, least likely to arouse suspicion. Although he did not miss a chance with younger women or even men, the murder template was established: see them at home, rather than the rooms, sitting in a lounge chair and offer an injection or take a blood specimen. Then walk out and call the relatives to say that she had died suddenly from something like heart failure, return to the rooms and backdate the computer records to justify the condition.

While it may have been a refinement of the procedure to kill a woman sitting in a lounge chair, it cannot be ignored that this was a precise analogue with the image of his dying mother in the chair at the window, gasping in pain for breath and heaving a sigh at the temporary relief of the morphine.

In retrospect it seems incredible that Shipman was not detected sooner; he would go into a room with a healthy and alert patient, in no apparent distress or discomfort, and walk out to announce that she, and occasionally he, had died. The word did spread among some staff and patients that he had a high death rate, but this was seen as a consequence of the elderly population he specialised in treating and, in any event, his reputation for unflagging devotion made any suggestion of foul play seem heretical. And Shipman constantly writhed under the possibility of scrutiny which drove him to hastily leave the group practice and set up on his own.

Another misconception is that Shipman was above the trappings of serial killers: sex and money. Some interesting anecdotes about sexually inappropriate remarks to female patients suggest he had difficulty with boundaries. In the case of Bianka Pomfret, an older woman who had bipolar disorder (manic depression), he formed a symbiotic liaison. It was never confirmed if this was sexual, but she eventually made out her will to him. It was only a sudden flare-up between them that gave her an insight into who she was dealing with and the last-minute inclination to change her will. This, however, did not save her from being killed.

In fact, as time went on, Shipman began amassing goods—jewellery, other personal items and money—pilfered from victims for trophy purposes. Another talisman was his beloved tortoise-shell fountain pen, with which he always wrote out the death certificates of his victims. It will remain a matter of speculation whether the forged Grundy will was some feeble, irrational hope to finance a departure from the practice, possibly a move to Europe, or even some other escape.

As the evidence unfolds, Shipman loses his aura and resembles a typical Brittain killer:[1] the pathological and intensely conflicted relationship with his mother; the grim obsessional need for control; the pseudo-moralising elitism; the polite, seemingly obsequious façade; the souvenirs; the bizarre marital set-up, with home a microcosm, albeit a safe one, of his insistence on total control. It reflects the arbitrary nature of obsessional control; for example, becoming incensed if the chairs are moved around the table but being unperturbed about sweeping dirt under a carpet. The Shipman home also says a lot about Primrose, who seems chronically depressed, focusing on her husband first, kids second and eating compulsively while the mess around her piles up—a metaphor for her state of mind. As it is with Shipman whose control of patients, staff, everyone, alternates with the mess at home, just like his mind. What started perhaps inadvertently, accidentally or impulsively, became habitual, then compulsive, ultimately thrilling and all-encompassing.

Even more troubling is the notion that Shipman simply considered the patients he killed to be a bothersome irrelevance. There is plenty of evidence that he despised his patients, many of whom worshipped him—his offer to put up a plaque over the chair of his victim Ivy Lomas being just one example. This was really a desperate, pathetic comment about a patient, especially as he always presented himself as the ultimate caring physician. Shipman, in short, did not need a motive to kill his patients. When they became too tedious, annoying, or unable to match his need for adulation, he just resolved it in the most clinical and indifferent fashion.

There is much more to be learned about Britain's most prolific serial killer, and—so far—the world's worst medical serial killer. Shipman defies comparison with killers such as Englishman Dennis Nilson (who murdered fifteen men and boys) or American Jeffrey Dahmer (who murdered seventeen men and boys) but has an unnerving similarity with Reginald John Christie, the murderer of 10 Rillington Place. Christie killed his victims for sex. A pathological liar, he attributed his activities to an incident when he was nine. Viewing his grandmother's open coffin at the undertaker, he became highly aroused. Shipman too was highly affected by the death of his mother when he was young and impressionable. Christie would win his victim's trust by offering them medical help (including abortion), using first aid skills he had learned in the ambulance corps. He stunned his victims using the household gas supply before strangling them and then having sex with their fresh corpses. There are elements in Christie's approach that mirror the Munchausen syndrome, where patients go to extraordinary lengths to fake symptoms to ensure treatment in hospital. Such patients invariably experience serious illness during their upbringing, either in themselves or a relative.

Furthermore, they or their parents may have worked in a medical role, as a nurse or ambulance officer. The Munchausen patient, driven by a pathological rage, has an astonishing, irresistible attraction to the powerful role of the healer. If they cannot be the healer, then they forge a symbiotic alliance by becoming a perennial patient. Shipman and Christie can be seen as mirror images—offering to help but turning their rage on to the hapless patient victims.

Shipman is credited with killing at least 250 patients. Swango was implicated in up to 60 sudden and unexplained deaths of patients. The similarity between the two is eerie. Swango operated in hospital environments; Shipman did his killing in the patients' homes, sometimes in his rooms.

Of all the medical serial killers, Shipman's zone of operation causes the most concern. Killing in hospitals permitted Swango to get away with a certain amount of mayhem before being detected. However, this is nothing compared to the risks that lie in the suburbs, doctors' rooms and homes of the community when a doctor who derives a thrill from killing is let loose. Shipman exploited these spaces to the fullest, and everything possible needs to be learned about his methods, which will not go unnoticed by his successors.

Shipman is all too easy to dismiss as a serial killer who just became addicted to doing it quickly and easily with the convenient use of heroin. The paradox of Shipman's medical role is that it reveals, as nothing else has done, the utter loss of the human element that is so crucial to the engagement between doctor and patient.

In 1957 Wertham described the Orestes complex to explain some cases of matricide: murder of the mother, a mostly rare crime. Wertham used the term *catathymic process* to describe a sexually immature but homosexually orientated son trapped in a dependent but hostile relationship with a possessive mother. The murderers came from large mother-dominated families with hostile, absent or rejecting fathers. The murderer would have extremely high dependency on the mother associated with intermittent feelings of failure. Feelings of aggression, pain and dysphoria (painful emotions like depression) would be projected on to the victim. To make matters worse, there were case reports of mothers who had engaged in sexually explicit behaviour, if not overt seduction, of their sons.

The killing occurred in response to intense emotional conflicts—the catathymic crisis—that led the offenders to believe they had to carry out a violent act to relieve the tension. The conflict arose from fears of intimacy or sexual inadequacy. Typically, the murders were sudden, shockingly violent acts carried out on a close relative such as the mother. In technical terms, there is a seemingly unsolvable psychic state of tension (called 'an incubation period'), projection of responsibility for the internal tension on to an external agency—that is, the victim—and the perception that violence was the only means of resolution. Like a suicide, the homicide was an attempt to escape the situation of entrapment. After a period of internal conflict and rumination, the violent act was carried out.

In plain language, the offender would become preoccupied with the victim over a period to the point of fixation, developing a tremendous urge to kill. This was followed by a release of tension, a sense of relief and even a change of attitude towards the victim. Further study established that the offender had an intolerable need for control—and the ultimate form of control is abandonment. This they had, in reality or fantasy, experienced at the hand of their mother. By killing, they attempted to reverse the loss of control. Furthermore, without insight into the underlying psychological issues, they would offend again.

It became clear that not only matricide could occur in response to a catathymic crisis, but fathers, lovers or people usually unknown to the killer could also be victims. This was described as a displacement to other people as a substitute for the figure at whom the murderous impulses were directed, often thought to be a similar mechanism to that affecting sadistic serial killers.

Now consider Shipman. He is deeply attached to his mother, who returns his feelings accordingly—they are described in the family as being 'like twins'. Whether actual incest occurred will never be known, but the knowledge of the thirteen-year-old boy, showing signs of premature puberty, sleeping in the same bed, suggests a considerable blurring of boundaries. While his father was not violent or brutal, he seems to have been pushed out by the two, and probably reacted accordingly by focusing on his own interests, as well as on the other children.

Then, at the vulnerable time when he is in his final year of school, Shipman's mother gets lung cancer. For the few months she has left, he would rush back from school to see her turn from the window where she sits, proffer herself to the doctor's needle and fall back with a sigh as the narcotic relief washes through her.

She dies and Shipman is utterly grief-stricken, running all night through the town streets to deaden his pain. After that, he is guarded, walled-off, inaccessible to people. Before long, he is trapped in a marriage with parental responsibilities that only adds to his simmering anger. This he tries to stifle with pethidine, but it is only a partial solution and one that nearly leads to the end of his career.

In Shipman's mind there was an irreconcilable nexus between his attachment to his mother, his rage at being abandoned by her through death, his further anger at being trapped by his wife and his utter inability to have any control over his domestic situation. By the time he finished medical school, the externalisation, displacement and projection are complete. Patients, especially women, who need him, are first seduced by his devotion, then dispatched in the one manner he knows— the swift lulling relief of a heroin overdose. He did it again and again, addictively repeating the displaced rage towards his mother and making them all, every single one of them, pay for what she had done to him. Shipman did not kill his mother, but he could never forgive her for deserting him the way she did. He identified with the escape she obtained from narcotic injections when dying of cancer; he displaced his rage by killing his patient victims. He was already set on a medical career by the time his mother died, but the boundary between caring and killing was no different than the conflict between the adoration and rage his mother had induced in him, and left him to deal with on his own.

It was truly an Orestes syndrome of staggering proportions and the wretched fate of his patients that Shipman was able to follow a medical career and embark on an unheralded clinicide. Had he been forced to find his victims in the wider world, rather than the assembly-line delivery of a medical practice, he would have been caught years earlier.

Shipman's public image of suburban father and parent was a protective screen, but how much consolation did it provide him? Did he consider himself to be leading a life of quiet desperation? Some extremely vicious serial killers have managed this. Later, when caught, they expressed regret for letting down their families without so much as a backward glance at their victims, an example of the pseudo-morality that courses through their thinking.

But Shipman's relationship with Primrose remains perplexing. Were they bonded by the silent but undisclosed fact of her awareness of what he was doing? Would a wife, stumbling on the knowledge that her husband was murdering his patients, remain numb and silent, fearful that she would be next? Or did she become an inadvertent ally, sharing his loathing of 'them'—the ever-demanding, grasping and insufficiently grateful patients? Together Shipman and Primrose seem like a couple bound by pullulating resentment: of their background, of the families they despised, of the doctors who thought they were not socially good enough, of the patients who could never understand how good their doctor was and how lucky they were to have him. As yet, there are no answers to these puzzles.

The public domain, mediated by tabloid papers and talkback radio, had no doubt about Shipman: he was evil, pure and simple. But this is of no use whatsoever. If the moral concept of evil is ever shown to be viable, there is a clear and unambiguous case that someone axiomatically evil like Shipman would lose the right to be allowed to live. But granting Shipman this privilege merely allows him to escape a poorly barbed hook and feed his sense of exceptionalism. The most enduring debate in forensic psychiatry is whether psychopaths are born or made. The consensus is that psychopaths are born bad, and will become bad if given the chance. In bald terms, there is as much chance that a psychopath will have a conscience (or can be helped to find one), as there is of a fish riding a bicycle. Shipman did not care in the slightest about his victims or what he did to them. He was born this way, his mother's early death at a vulnerable time was a trigger and template, and his destiny was ineluctable until the moment of his death.

There are no satisfactory answers. We can only attempt to demount Shipman from the pedestal of some sort of elegant clinical terminator, injudiciously killing his patients in a rebarbative euthanasia, to just another killer who deserves nothing more than the refrain that if he was one of us, then he was barely so, and scarcely that. What an awful sod.

8

More medical murder

Dr John Bodkin Adams, Dr Arnfinn Nesset and Dr Mario Jascalevich

To kill a relative of whom you are tired is something. But to inherit his property afterwards, that is genuine pleasure.

Honoré de Balzac

It is no offence to his victims to describe Shipman's modus operandi as a mordant assembly-line process. His victims were mostly elderly women with chronic diseases. They were unwell but mostly ambulant and seldom terminal. Involved in his near-manic daily schedule of consultations and home visits, Shipman would see them, kill them and move on. Shipman was no bureaucratic cog in a vast political killing machine but a necrophiliac serial killer serving an inner drive to meet an extreme need for control and power.

When the news of Shipman's murderous career emerged, many people thought of John Bodkin Adams, the doctor who was widely believed to have killed at least 132 patients, and actually got away with it. Many of his patients died soon after changing their wills in favour of their doctor. Adams inherited money, cars, jewellery and antique furniture from all 132 patients. Such is the controversy over his culpability that debate still rages, fuelled by the release of closed files in 2003.

If you were to ask Agatha Christie to write a play about a doctor killing his patients—in a setting involving sexual politics, hypocrisy, deception, manipulation and extraordinary greed extending to the rich, the famous, the titled and the powerful; and the murderer, with an extensive web of influence going to the highest in the land, mixing with lawyers, clergymen, politicians and theatrical folk at solemn church services, sumptuous picnics, shooting parties and elegant dinners—you would have difficulty believing that such a scenario was true. And yet, Adams's case study shows that life is always more bizarre than fiction, and what happened at a peaceful English coastal resort could not have been made up.

John Bodkin Adams was born in County Antrim in January 1899. The family were members of the secretive fundamentalist sect, the Plymouth Brethren, and he continued his association with the group all his life. His father, a watchmaker and lay preacher, and younger brother died while he was in his teens. He had a close relationship with his mother, Ellen, and lived with her until she died in 1943.

A mediocre student, Adams graduated in medicine in 1921 in Belfast. It soon became apparent that he was not specialist material and he moved to England to work in a Bristol practice where the partners started the day with prayers. Shortly afterwards he moved to the south-east coastal town of Eastbourne, a retirement haven for many wealthy retired couples, and especially for widows.

Adams bought into the Emerson, Gurney and Rainey practice in College Road, renting a home near the railway station. His progress up the social ladder was rapid. In 1922, he did his rounds on a bicycle. By 1926, he had a Renault two-seater coupe with a chauffeur. Ten years later he was a senior partner in the practice, living in a large house on Seaside Road, and his practice had grown to 2000 patients. By 1956, the year before his trial, one source listed him as the richest doctor in England.

In 1933 Adams became engaged to Norah O'Hara, the daughter of a wealthy butcher. Her parents bought them a house in Carew Road as a present, but the relationship foundered the following year and the engagement was called off. One view is his mother, determined to hang on to her son, refused to let him marry into 'trade'. Another factor is that Adams was homosexual and spent the rest of his life as a professional bachelor. Any doubts about this were confirmed by Patricia Cullen who showed his involvement, in particular, with two influential men in the town: Sir Roland Gwynne, a magistrate and former mayor of the town, whose brother was the local MP; and, Alexander Seekings, the deputy constable of Eastbourne. But Adams must have been fond of Norah O'Hara, whom he later remembered in his will.

In 1934 Adams became a part-time anaesthetist at the voluntary Princess Alice Memorial Hospital, where he frequently ate cake, fell asleep in the middle of operations and muddled procedures. Although this caused the surgeons considerable annoyance, in the gentlemanly spirit that prevailed at the time nothing was ever done. Noting his endomorphic stature (he was of a heavy build), raises the question of sleep apnoea, a condition which is associated with sleep-related crime.

As a doctor, Adams had automatic entry to the town's leading social activities. He joined the Wine and Food Society, the Camera Club and the Rifle Club. He was on the YMCA committee and ran Bible classes. He always bought the latest model camera, had the best collection of sporting guns in the area, and was a regular guest at exclusive social gatherings.

A significant number of Eastbourne's population was over 65, and were financially comfortable, if not wealthy, by the standards of the time. They tended to be widows and lived on their own in mansion blocks, big old houses or luxury hotels. They were undoubtedly lonely for the company of men, but in those days it was considered scandalous if an unaccompanied man was seen going into their home unless he was a priest or a doctor.

At five foot nine and one hundred and seventy-five pounds, balding and pink-jowled with stubby hands and round spectacles, Adams was not an imposing physical presence, but he had a convincing bedside manner. His religious faith and Irish charm had a constant appeal to his patients. He read the Bible in the surgery and had a wall plaque that said 'Rest In The Lord' over his bed. He would leave religious tracts in the sickroom, and could even fall on his knees to pray before entering a patient's bedroom—one patient provided him with a kneeler on her landing. He would come into the room, lay his hand over that of the patient, and ask in his soft Irish brogue how she was feeling.

This was an age when doctoring was as much about reassurance as it was about relief of symptoms. Before World

War II there were no antibiotics to treat infections, and medications to treat conditions such as high blood pressure were crude preparations compared to the refined and effective medicines now available. Drugs we take for granted to treat insomnia and anxiety, such as benzodiazepines, were unknown. Sedatives used included bromides, chloral hydrate, barbiturates and morphine preparations; all of these drugs were highly addictive, had serious side effects and could easily cause death by stopping respiration. Yet patients needed their suffering alleviated, and the doctor's visit was a feature of the treatment. Adams knew his patients wanted reassurance and he often kept bad news from them and used placebos.

At the time, it was not uncommon for patients to remember doctors in their wills, and Adams received regular bequests. In 1935 Matilda Whitton left him £7000—a considerable amount by today's standards. Her family contested the will but Adams, regarding the legacy as his by right, fought the case in the High Court and won.

Adams was not afraid to give his patients high doses of drugs, and it was widely known that he had a high mortality rate. Balancing this was the fact that many of his patients were elderly and ailing. But the speed at which old women died after willing their money to him was striking—especially when it turned out that the wills had been altered so the old ladies were cremated instead of buried as originally stipulated. The matter became the talk of Eastbourne and people began to speculate about the deaths of other patients. It was whispered that Adams did his rounds with a bottle of morphine in one pocket and a blank will form in the other. There were stories of his visits to banks with patients to change their wills, of previously healthy patients who died suddenly after adding codicils to their wills in favour of Adams, and of patients becoming addicted to medication he prescribed.

A wealthy steel merchant, William Mawhood, used to invite Adams on pheasant shoots and lent him money to buy Kent Lodge, his imposing Victorian villa in Seaside Road. As Mawhood lay dying, his wife Edith overheard Adams at the deathbed asking to be left the estate in exchange for looking after his wife. Mrs Mawhood, to her lasting credit, chased him out of the room with her walking stick.

Adams's ruthless pursuit of legacies remained a subject of discussion in the community. He seems to have charged many private patients only nominal fees on the understanding that he would be rewarded in their wills, not an unusual practice among Eastbourne doctors. But Adams would ring up the solicitor to check that provision had been made for him in a patient's will. (He was said to have rung up once from a patient's deathbed.) He also liked patients to give him silver.

Adams would take patients to London specialists, paying the specialist in cash so that he could add a few pounds to his own bill to the patient. However, he did not charge many poorer patients who adored him. Dr Basil Barkworth, who worked in the practice, said that Adams did not hide his wealth and was criticised by the partners for his profligate use of narcotics and for sending bills to NHS patients.

These practices earned him the dislike of most of the other Eastbourne doctors, perhaps adding to his determination to become richer than any of them. After 1950 he included among his patients the duke of Devonshire, the high sheriff of Sussex and the chief constable of Eastbourne.

Rumours continued to multiply. Adams visited Clara Neil-Miller, an elderly spinster, the night before she died. A resident of the nursing home told police she went into the bedroom after Adams left to find the windows wide open on a winter night, bedclothes thrown back over the bedrail and Miss Neil-Miller naked, her nightdress folded back to her neck. Adams put coronary thrombosis on the death certificate; the post-mortem indicated she died of pneumonia.

It was the death of his patient Edith Morrell (81) that led to Adams being charged with murder. A wealthy woman, she owned a ten-room mansion and a Rolls Royce. Suffering a lingering stroke, Mrs Morrell was not expected to live more than a year, but in fact survived for two and a half years and was cremated at her own request, the ashes scattered over the English Channel.

Adams met Edith Morrell two years before her death when she was at the Olinda Nursing Home. He attended her regularly and moved her to a nursing home across the road from his practice. Mrs Morrell made several wills. In some of them, Adams received large sums of money or furniture—in others, he was not mentioned. On 24 August 1949 she added a clause saying that Adams would receive nothing. Mrs Morrell must have changed her mind again as Adams contacted her solicitor, telling him she wanted a codicil added to her will that left him a case of silver and a Rolls Royce. The solicitor contacted his client, the codicil was confirmed and signed.

At 10 p.m. on 12 November 1950, Adams attended the ailing Mrs Morrell, surprising the night nurse caring for her. Mrs Morrell was in severe distress, struggling to breathe. Adams insisted the nurse give her a large injection of morphine, followed by a second one if she became restless; at 2 a.m., shortly after the second shot, Mrs Morrell died. The nurse claimed Adams had given her a massive overdose.

Edith Morrell left an estate of £157,000, of which Adams received a silver chest valued at £275 and an old Rolls Royce which he drove around Eastbourne. Flaunting his new-found wealth led to a new outbreak of gossip, setting first the media, then the police, into action.

Alfred and Gertrude Hullett died within months of each other in 1956. Adams had given Gertrude Hullett the medication that could have caused her death which was certified by him as suicide. He had treated 71-year-old Mr Hullett, who had bowel cancer, before he died in March 1956, putting the cause of death on the death certificate as coronary thrombosis.

Hullett left an estate of some £266,000 with a bequest of £3000 to Adams. On Mrs Hullett's death soon after in July, Adams received a Rolls Royce which he sold for £8400, the rest of the estate going to Mrs Hullett's daughter. The local coroner, Dr Sommerville, suspected that Mrs Hullett's apparent suicide was murder and brought in Scotland Yard. The Hulletts's bodies were exhumed; the autopsies revealed the presence of legally prescribed painkillers and tranquillisers. Adams said he had prescribed these drugs during treatment.

The Murder Squad, led by Superintendent Hannam, examined the deaths of 400 of Adams's patients over twenty years. Police estimated the flow of bequests was worth £3000 a year to the GP. Detective Chief Superintendent Charles Hewitt of Scotland Yard came to believe that Adams killed as many as 25 patients by injecting them with large doses of morphine and 'eased' many others to death after influencing them to leave him something in their wills.

This flagrantly self-interested interpretation of the law persuaded Attorney-General Sir Reginald Manningham-Buller QC, that he need only put Dr Bodkin Adams in the witness box to find him guilty. After a rival newspaper broke the story that the doctor was a suspect, London journalist Percy

Hoskins, crime reporter for *The Express*, became convinced that Adams was innocent. In the teeth of widespread media claims accusing Adams, he exposed a police campaign, revealing that Scotland Yard planted anti-Adams stories in national newspapers.

In 1957, the police decided to charge Adams with murdering Edith Morrell and Gertrude Hullett. Following his arrest, Adams, after exclaiming that Edith Morell 'wanted to die' said: 'That cannot be murder. It is impossible to accuse a doctor.'

What followed was the longest murder trial in English criminal history, the first trial of a doctor accused of murdering his patients since that of Dr William Palmer in 1856. That it allegedly happened while he was treating them—'easing the passing' in Adams's oily phrase—caused a sensation.

When John Bodkin Adams stood trial at the Old Bailey on 18 March 1957, charged with the murder of Mrs Edith Morrell, the prosecution's case looked totally damning. Nurses who had attended Mrs Morrell stated that Adams had prescribed massive doses of painkillers. These drugs were unnecessary because the patient was in no pain. What the prosecution did not know was that the nurses' missing report books were in the hands of the defence. How they had been discovered remains a matter of contention. The report books showed that no morphine had been given on its own, and the reported 'large injection' was a mild sedative, given to Mrs Morrell when she was fully conscious. Six years after her death, the nurses' memories could not be relied on.

During the trial, Adams spoke only the words, 'I am not guilty, my Lord', and did not testify. The defence case was that everyone had to die sometime, so doctors should do what they could to 'ease the passing'. Adams's barrister, Geoffrey Lawrence QC, systemically annihilated the prosecution's case.

When he cross-examined the nurses it became obvious that they were giving evidence based on their recollection of events. However, they admitted they had made written records of the doctor's instructions regarding administration of medication. The records produced, each written up by the nurse on duty at the time, completely refuted their evidence.

In his summing-up, Justice Devlin made a crucial distinction. If treatment was given, however well-meaning, with the intention of killing a patient, it was murder. But if treatment intended to relieve pain had the incidental effect of shortening the life of the patient, it need not be murder. But even then, Adams could have claimed to be 'relieving pain and suffering' to get away with it. It took the jury just 44 minutes to find Adams not guilty.

The case of murdering the Hulletts was promptly dropped. Adams was later found guilty on fourteen charges of forging prescriptions, forging documents that allowed medicine and surgical equipment to be falsely delivered, not revealing a financial interest when signing cremation orders, and forging other documents. He was fined and barred from practising.

Despite being found not guilty, many people believed Adams had got away with murder and some newspapers voiced their doubts. Adams successfully sued several publishers for defamation, receiving large sums of money and ensuring there was no further discussion until his death. He would send Percy Hoskins a yearly card thanking him for 'another year of my life'.

Adams was restored to the British medical register in 1961 and returned to practice in Eastbourne, welcomed back by many patients. He kept a lower profile, but a bequest in 1965 revived old memories. In his later years, he virtually gave up private practice, devoting his time to anaesthetics.

Adams died after a fall at his home in July 1983, and, like many of his patients, was cremated. The large estate of £402,970 only confirmed the views of many that he had benefited unfairly from the wills of his patients. Among the remaining items sold at auction was his old brass ivory-handled syringe. He left Percy Hoskins about £1500. He allowed his former fiancée Miss O'Hara first choice of his possessions, indicating his lingering sentiment for her.

After his death, the media was able to discuss the case without restraint. It was claimed that Adams had killed several hundred patients and the police had prepared murder charges on fewer than nine of his patients. Dr John Surtees, who wrote about the case, said that Adams was from a different culture. He was genuinely concerned to help his patients, but at the same time completely amoral in his approach. He believed that his poorer private patients should receive their drugs on the NHS, and was not above forging other doctors' signatures to procure them.

Author Richard Gordon once met Adams in Torremolinos. He described him as a chatty, jolly, beefy-faced, moon-spectacled man in a trilby hat, organising bridge games for adoring widows.

In 1985, in an unprecedented breach of judicial convention, Lord Devlin (as he became) published *Easing the Passing* on the Adams trial, giving his opinion that although insufficient evidence was produced to convict Adams, he could be described as a greedy mercy-killer.

Adams experienced severe loss during his teenage years with the death of his father and brother. He had an over-dependent relationship with his mother and there is the impression that his one attempt to escape her clutches was the engagement to Norah O'Hara, which she sabotaged; by the time she died, it was too late for him. His over-pious religious behaviour reflected a sort of pseudo-morality and it is likely that at some level he saw himself as a mission killer. Bearing in mind that homosexuality was strictly prohibited and could lead to criminal conviction, it must have reinforced his view of himself as an outsider leading a double life.

Social factors played a significant role in Adams's behaviour. In the class-ridden English society of the time, when medical practice was especially snobbish, he came from a humble background. He would have been well aware, both at medical school and later in practice, of his marginality in the old-school-tie network. His involvement with Gwynne and Seekings fed the belief that there was a different set of rules for those in the Establishment, and the rest of the population. It appears he over-compensated for this with extraordinary venality and a determination to not only have the best of everything but make sure everyone else knew about it. By gouging fees and manipulating patients to leave him bequests in their wills, he was immoral and manipulative, reflecting a narcissism that entitled him to put his needs before those of anyone else. Despite exploiting his patients, Adams maintained a fantastically loyal following who responded to his charismatic use of a combination of reassurance, flattery and magicianship.

The enduring impression left by Adams is that of pathetic rage. Time and time again, Adams shoved the old ladies (and a few men as well) across the line to a premature death. Easing the passing? Hardly. As he banged the plunger down the syringe, was he remembering the bondage to his mother and the rage he felt when she ended the engagement, the one chance he had to escape before she died? The old ladies were the only recourse to inflate his limited self-esteem and he certainly made them pay for it.

Much as commentators assumed that Adams was a bizarre but quaint interlude, unlikely to recur, future events showed that this was a complacent illusion. Clinicide continued but mostly remained below the horizon. Several disparate cases emerged, having little impact except, of course, in the locality they occurred. One such case is Norwegian hospital administrator, Dr Arnfinn Nesset, the worst serial killer in Scandinavia. Nesset may have killed as many as 138 patients with curare (a short-acting muscle relaxant drug) over a five-year period in the late 1970s, reportedly obtaining sexual satisfaction while watching them die.

The Orkdal Valley Nursing Home opened during 1977, and had a high mortality rate. Between 1977 and 1980, 30 patients died. In early 1981, local journalists received a tip that Nesset had ordered large quantities of curacit, a derivative of curare, which is usually given as a muscle relaxant in surgery. In lethal doses, it causes a slow, painful death. It breaks down rapidly after entering the body and is very difficult to detect post-mortem.

The publicity led first administrators, then authorities, to investigate the matter, their inquiries focusing on 46-year-old Nesset, described as a balding, bespectacled, mild-mannered man.[1] An illegitimate child, Nesset was brought up in a remote rural community. As an adult, he had feelings of inferiority and rejection.

Nesset claimed that he intended to use the curacit to put down his dog. This alibi broke down on the grounds that he had obtained enough curacit to kill at least 200 people and he did not own a dog. He then confessed to murdering 27 patients between May 1977 and November 1980. 'I've killed so many I'm unable to remember them all,' he told police, prompting them to check lists of patients who died in three institutions where Nesset had worked since 1962. Investigators thought there were 62 victims, but autopsies were pointless since curacit disappears over time. Nesset was charged with killing 25 of the Orkdal Valley patients, five counts of forgery and embezzlement of 1800 kroner from his victims.

Four psychiatrists found that he was sane and fit for trial. However, shortly before the trial in October 1982, Nesset suddenly recanted his confession. He claimed different motives for the murders including mercy killing and sexual pleasure from the act of killing.

At the trial the prosecution claimed that his motive was financial as he had stolen money from all of his victims. Nesset pleaded innocent on all counts and said he had heard voices telling him to kill the patients. He claimed he had taken the money for missionary and charity use. His lawyers put to the jury that Nesset was mentally unbalanced, citing as defences insanity (schizophrenia), euthanasia, as well as morbid pleasure in the act of killing, presumably on the basis that they had nothing to lose by covering the field.

Judges were unmoved by the defence plea that Nesset considered himself a 'demigod', holding the power of life and death over his elderly patients. On 11 March 1983, Nesset was convicted on 22 counts of murder, one count of attempted murder, plus five counts of forgery and embezzlement. He was given the maximum sentence possible under Norwegian law: 21 years in prison, with a possibility of ten more years' preventive detention.

The muscle relaxant drugs that Nesset used were widely available in a range of preparations and easy to obtain. Predominantly used for anaesthesia, they were administered by injection or intravenous drip. Injected into an unventilated patient away from the operating theatre, the muscle relaxants caused muscular paralysis, the patient would be unable to breathe and suffocate horribly. Because they could not move or speak, there was no way they could attract attention. Afterwards, as they had remained still, the body would look undisturbed and there was nothing to suggest anything violent had occurred. Furthermore, the drugs were hard to detect in the body with the technology at that time.

Muscle relaxants have no addictive potential and the idea of misuse, let alone facilitation of murder, would not have occurred to anyone in the usual course of events. No one could train in medicine without being made aware of the dangers of incorrect use of these drugs. These facts did not pass unnoticed to those who had their minds on the opposite side of the medical role in saving life—namely, the promotion of death.

A similar type of clinicide is that of Dr Mario E. Jascalevich who also injected patients with curare. Jascalevich, described as a slightly built, bespectacled man, was born in Buenos Aires in 1927. In 1955, he emigrated to the United States and commenced an internship at Passaic General Hospital, New Jersey. He joined Riverdell Hospital in Oradell, New Jersey in 1962.

Jascalevich specialised in surgery and developed a surgical stapler for suturing wounds. He did not have good relationships with his colleagues and was thought to be jealous of their success. Two colleagues, Dr Stanley Harris and Dr Allan Lans, suspected Jascalevich murdered patients with curare to make his own post-operative morbidity and mortality figures look better by comparison. In 1966 eighteen empty vials of curare were found in Jascalevich's locker. Confronted with the vials, Jascalevich claimed he had been using the drugs in experiments on dying dogs at Seton Hall Medical School in Jersey City, where he had a teaching position.

In November 1966, Bergen County authorities launched an investigation into nine suspicious deaths at Riverdell Hospital. In each case, patients were admitted to the hospital for surgery and died of unrelated causes, before or after 'minor' elective surgical procedures. However, the case was rejected by a grand jury, and no action could be taken.

For the next ten years, rumours about Jascalevich continued to circulate. In January 1976 the *New York Times* ran a series of articles about 'Doctor X' suspected of murdering patients. A month prior to the case being reopened, New York Deputy Medical Examiner Dr Michael Baden supplied an affidavit to the Superior Court in Bergen County stating that at least a score of patients who died at Riverdell in 1966 succumbed for other reasons than those stated on their death certificates. A Superior Court judge gave the prosecutor the right to exhume the bodies of five Riverdell Hospital patients who had died days after routine surgical procedures between December 1965 and September 1966. The tissue specimens were tested with the new techniques of radioimmunoassay (RIA) and high performance liquid chromatography (HPLC) to detect the presence of poison. Finally, they had proof. Formally accused of slaying patients Savino, Henderson, Rohrbeck, Biggs and Arzt, Jascalevich surrendered his medical licence.

On 28 February 1978, eighteen jurors were chosen for what was to become one of the longest criminal trials in US history. Two murder charges were dropped for lack of evidence. The defence focused on the long-term stability of curare under the conditions to which the bodies were subjected between 1966 and 1976. Defence witnesses testified that curare could not survive in embalmed bodies for ten years. It was contended that RIA and HPLC were relatively new procedures and could not be used to detect curare in human tissue.

On 24 October 1978, after 34 weeks of testimony, Jascalevich was acquitted of all murder charges. He faced several malpractice suits and fought a court battle to get reinstated on the medical register. He later returned to his native Argentina and died of a cerebral haemorrhage in September 1984. The case of the curare deaths at Riverdell remains officially unsolved.

Clinicide was there, surfacing above the waterline at intervals and showing no indications that it was going to stop.

9

Murdering the madam

Both marriage and death ought to be welcome: the one
promises happiness, doubtless the other assures it.

Mark Twain, Letters

The majority of murders are domestic. Offenders kill someone
known to them, usually in their family. The official term for
this is *uxorious homicide*. As generic murderers, doctors are
no different and most often kill their partners. To do this, they
have an advantage on the rest of the population in having
access to the means to do so. One of the earliest documented
cases is that of Dr Thomas Smethurst. At the age of 24, he
married a woman two decades his senior. As a practitioner
Smethurst had some success promoting the water cure (as in
spas), running a clinic in Surrey, publishing a book and editing

a journal. By 1858 while living with his wife in a Bayswater boarding house, he began an affair with the younger Isabella Banks. Evicted by his wife from the boarding house, he and Isabella moved into Richmond, having gone through a bigamous marriage ceremony. The following year Isabella died after two months of severe gastrointestinal illness, leaving a sum of £100 to Smethurst. The two doctors who attended her during the illness believed that she had been given an 'irritant' poison and reported the matter to a magistrate. Smethurst was arrested and charged with murder.

A forensic expert, Dr Swaine Taylor, found arsenic in Isabella's stools and in a bottle of mouthwash in Smethurst's possession. However, cross-examined on his findings in court, Taylor admitted that his tests were contaminated and no arsenic was found in the victim's organs. Despite this, Smethurst was convicted by the jury and sentenced to death. The Home Secretary had the case reviewed and Smethurst was pardoned, only to be convicted of bigamy and spend a year in prison. On release, undeterred by his original conviction for murder, he successfully sued Isabella's relatives for his share of the will.

The courtroom failure of Dr Taylor, promoted as an expert in toxicology, was a media spectacle, and his forensic career ended in a humiliating fashion. This set a pattern that has continued up to the present: the rise and fall of the charismatic forensic expert, courted by lawyers, judges and the media, becoming an undisputable authority in their own right, only to come to dismal failure through a series of botched judgements.

To a psychopath, murder is the highest form of self-fulfilment. Such personalities have a grandiose self-image, engage in feckless self-promotion and make ideal con men. A good example of a rampaging psychopath in medicine is that of Dr Edward William Pritchard. Born in 1825, Pritchard served as a surgeon in the Royal Navy for six years but was persuaded by his wife to settle down in a Yorkshire practice. He made himself popular by writing articles in the local paper but ran into debt and had to sell the practice after six years. Pritchard then decamped to Glasgow, where he antagonised colleagues by giving lectures about implausible adventures and travels.

On the home front, Pritchard's fondness for tumbling nursemaids led to two dying in unusual circumstances. Extending his range, Pritchard then poisoned his wife and mother-in-law with antimony that he bought at a local pharmacy. Several doctors became involved, suspicion was aroused and he was charged with murder and found guilty. Although Pritchard confessed his guilt before the execution in 1865, the motive remained unclear. He has the distinction of being the last person to be publicly hanged in Scotland.

Fast forward a century to the case of Dr Geza De Kaplany, a 36-year-old anaesthetist who lived in San Jose, California. De Kaplany had done his medical training in Hungary but came to the United States as a refugee after the Russian invasion in 1956.

After a very brief courtship, he married Hajne Piller in early 1962. Hajne and her mother had also fled Hungary after the invasion. Described as an astonishing beauty, Hajne won some beauty competitions and then worked as a showgirl in a skimpy costume that made the most of her voluptuous charms.

But the marriage soon ran into problems because of De Kaplany's pathological jealousy. After a short honeymoon in Hawaii, the couple began to drift apart. De Kaplany came to believe that Hajne was promiscuous and would run off with another man. The situation was inflamed by a 'mutual friend' who fed gossip to De Kaplany that appeared to confirm his obsessive suspicions.

On the morning of 28 August 1962, De Kaplany and Hajne had sex. Then he tied her to the bed and attacked her, dousing her naked body, including her eyes and vagina, with acid and slicing open one breast. Hajne's screams were partially drowned by the sound of loud classical music and running bathwater. The police were called to the apartment by neighbours disturbed by the noise and sounds of screaming. They found Hajne scorched with third-degree corrosive burns. The emergency medical team burned their hands on her acid-soaked body.

In De Kaplany's bedroom police found surgical gloves, knives, bottles of nitric, hydrochloric and sulphuric acid—the nitric acid bottle was two-thirds empty—surgical swabs, rolls of adhesive tape, coils of electrical cord and a bottle of whisky.

De Kaplany was arrested. Maintaining an aloof façade, he insisted that Hajne would live. He claimed that he was trying to 'erase' the beauty only he was allowed to possess. Hajne remained in hospital for 36 days before dying in agony.

Investigations revealed that De Kaplany was something of a fantasist. He only added the 'De' to his name after he left Hungary. He misled a biographer into believing that he was a hero of the Resistance against the communists before the 1956 invasion. In fact, he had done his medical studies under the communists, received support for training and left the country without difficulty, not under duress as a refugee.

De Kaplany had been in a number of relationships, but they seem to have been rather distant and ended unsatisfactorily. He had in fact married Hajne after less than three weeks' courtship after asking her mother for her hand in marriage.

Her mother, something of a snob, if not a reactionary, was impressed by De Kaplany's stories of noble descent and his old-world courtesy.

When the case came to trial in 1963, De Kaplany pleaded not guilty and remained calm during initial proceedings. But when photographic evidence of the crime was produced, he became hysterical and confessed his guilt, reversing his plea and claiming insanity.

Several defence psychiatrists called him schizophrenic, paranoid, a latent homosexual or a transvestite. However, the key testimony came from Dr Russell Lee, who played the court several hours of taped interviews in which De Kaplany claimed to have two personalities: the weak and unassertive Dr De Kaplany, and the strong husky 'Pierre La Roche'.

De Kaplany's case was going well. The media, public and the jurors were looking at him with some sympathy. Then Prosecutor Bergna flew in a surprise witness from Germany, Ruth Krueger, a former lover who had a son by him. She debunked De Kaplany's defence that he had a split personality, revealing him instead to be disingenuous, manipulative and deceitful.

Declared legally sane, De Kaplany was sentenced to life imprisonment and committed to a Californian prison medical facility. Taken away to start his sentence, his closing words to the press were: 'I am a dead man.'

If so, he was to demonstrate a remarkable resurrection. Six months before the date of his parole in 1975, De Kaplany was inexplicably released and smuggled to Taiwan to work as a heart specialist. The circumstances of his release caused a huge scandal, but he was never extradited and it remained unclear how the release had been organised. His subsequent fate is unknown.

Medicine can attract a certain kind of person who is lured by the power of life over death. This has an irresistible appeal to two personality types: psychopathic and narcissistic. Many clinicidal doctors have extremely narcissistic personalities, leading to a grandiose view of their own role and capabilities, and an inability to accept that they could be criticised or need assistance from others. That De Kaplany was paranoid is without doubt. It is almost impossible to estimate how far this drove him beyond losing contact with reality, leading him first to hideously mutilate and torture his wife with acid burns, then shuttle between denial and confession, changing defences during his trial in an attempt to protect his miserable hide.

Just to show that psychopaths who do not study the past are condemned to re-live it, albeit with the addition of a few twists from their particular psychopathology, there is psychiatrist Dr Colin Bouwer. Bouwer may not have been aware of his predecessor De Kaplany, but there are notable resonances with his case. He emigrated with his third wife, Annette, from his native South Africa to New Zealand. Having commenced an affair with a psychiatric colleague, he decided to murder his wife. It is unclear why Bouwer did not simply leave her and, typical of a psychopath, he simply followed his impulse to resolve the matter in the most convenient manner that came to mind, regardless of the consequences.

Bouwer started off as a general practitioner in South Africa, going on to work in psychiatry. From an early stage, there were accusations that he was abusing drugs and claiming false qualifications. He last worked at the Department of Psychiatry at Tygerberg Hospital in Cape Town. Here he was regarded with suspicion by colleagues and faced allegations of improper sexual relationships with patients by the time he left for New Zealand. He promptly got a position as a senior lecturer in psychiatry at the University of Otago in Dunedin.

On arrival, Bouwer exaggerated his qualifications, telling people that he had been a member of the ANC opposing the apartheid government. He claimed that he had refused to serve in the military, was detained without trial for six months and tortured by having wires attached to his genitals. None of this was true; Bouwer had served an unremarkable term as an army conscript.

Bouwer soon settled into the pleasant life of a senior medical lecturer in the southern town. The family appeared a model of conventionality, the parents and children going to watch sport and mixing with the neighbours. It did not take long before Bouwer had a series of affairs with nurses as well as a young psychiatrist. However, starting an affair with Dr Anne Walsh at a conference in Copenhagen prompted him to make plans to murder his wife.

Bouwer searched the internet to find information on drugs to kill his wife. He went to medical websites for information on a group of drugs known as sulphonylureas, used in the treatment of diabetes. He was specifically interested in finding out how sensitive toxicology testing was for detecting these drugs. Between 15 November 1999 and 5 January 2000 Bouwer purchased a number of hypoglycaemic drugs used in Type-2 (non-insulin dependent) diabetes. These drugs cause a precipitous drop in blood glucose levels causing coma and ultimately death without urgent intervention.

In November 1999 Annette Bouwer was admitted to hospital in a coma. She was diagnosed with hypoglycaemia (low blood sugar). On recovery she was advised to monitor blood glucose levels with a glucometer. She soon lapsed into a second coma. In December she had a partial pancreatectomy in an effort to lower her insulin levels. From then on her health declined rapidly until she died on 5 January 2000 at her home in Dunedin. The day before she died, Bouwer phoned his wife's family in South Africa telling them that Annette would be dead by the next day. He collected a final false prescription and arranged to be alone with Annette for an extended period while his children watched cricket on television at Dr Walsh's home.

Annette Bouwer's GP was preparing to write a death certificate listing an insulinoma as the cause of death until someone mentioned that Annette had believed someone was trying to poison her. Medical evidence suggested that Annette should have been admitted to hospital at least two days before she died. Given Bouwer's medical training, it appeared strange that he did not seek medical help sooner. This observation sparked inquiries pointing to murder. No insulinoma was found at autopsy, but tests revealed heavy concentrations of anti-diabetic drugs and sedatives.

After his wife's death, Bouwer continued teaching medical students at Otago University and maintained contact with Dr Walsh. Discussing the 'perfect murder' with the students, he said that he would inject a person between the toes. He went back to South Africa, emailing his lover to ask about the progress of the case against him.

Bouwer's arrogance, as expected, misled him. He thought the local police were too unsophisticated, if not stupid, to be able to prosecute a successful case against him. The police investigations discovered at least ten false scripts for sedative and anti-diabetic drugs after 30 September 1999 in names like 'Terrance Cairns' and 'B. McCollough'. They found a mortar and pestle with traces of sulphonylureas in Bouwer's home and traces of the drugs in the kitchen sink waste-disposal unit. Bouwer admitted to purchasing the drugs, but denied that he had caused his wife's death. He made the implausible claim that he had become depressed and obtained the drugs to kill himself but instead they were found and used by his wife to commit suicide. Other evidence revealed that he had also inquired about the ability of the Institute of Environmental Science and Research to detect sulphonylurea drugs.

As the pressure mounted, Bouwer's false claims multiplied. He said his wife had a neurological shunt but no such shunt was found at the autopsy. He claimed to have prostate cancer, but could not be examined as a result of his torture as an anti-apartheid activist in South Africa.

Through Interpol the investigating officers from New Zealand asked the South African police to investigate Dr Bouwer's background. The South African investigating team obtained statements from Dr Bouwer's family, in-laws, friends and colleagues. No medical records that he had hypoglycaemia or prostate cancer were found. To counter another one of his claims, the Office of the President of South Africa denied that Dr Bouwer had ever given medical treatment or advice to President Nelson Mandela as he had said on arrival in New Zealand.

In his application for bail, Bouwer alleged he had been detained and tortured in South Africa for six months in 1972; his first wife negated this. He said he had been raped by four men in South Africa; his family denied this. He said his wife was terminally ill in 1995; her family denied this. He said his first wife had killed herself and her children; the wife and children were alive and living in South Africa.

There were reports in the press from two former patients in South Africa who said Bouwer told them his wife was dying of cancer and then had sex with them. One patient said that in six months of treatment at Stikland Hospital in 1996, he came to her Tygerberg home twice for sex.

The six-week trial featured more than 150 witnesses, including several people in South Africa. During the trial it emerged that Bouwer was declared an impaired doctor by the South African Health Professions Council between 1981 and 1992. During that time, he was allowed to practise only under prescribed conditions, something he had failed to tell the New Zealand medical authorities.

To add to the already fantastic nature of the proceedings and show that, if nothing else, murder was a thriving family business in Clan Bouwer, the court heard that Dr Bouwer's son Colin junior (28), and his mother (Colin Bouwer senior's first wife) Mariette Kruger, were on trial for the murder of the son's wife Ria (23) in their Kempton Park home in Johannesburg on 7 May 1999.

It took the jury less than three hours to find that Bouwer senior killed his wife because of his affair with Anne Walsh and to obtain a substantial insurance payout. He was sentenced to life imprisonment in Christchurch, New Zealand. Bouwer unsuccessfully appealed his sentence, which saw the minimum non-parole period increased to fifteen years.

Meanwhile back in the homeland, Colin Bouwer junior, pleaded guilty to culpable homicide of his wife Ria during a heated argument after she threatened to leave with the children. She was found strangled in the guest bathroom of their home. Toiletries were strewn around the bathroom as if there had been a struggle. Her underwear was slashed in an attempt to make it appear that she had been sexually assaulted. In another attempt to throw police off the scent, their baby daughter, Melissa, was kidnapped by two armed men in March 2000. She was found, unhurt, a short time later.

Ria Bouwer's mother, Louise van Schalkwyk, had refused to accept police assurances that the crime was perpetrated by an outsider. She then hired a private investigator to crack the case, showing remarkable persistence despite being sent five straw voodoo dolls with moulded genitals, and having her leg broken by an attacker.

Colin Bouwer's mother, Mariette Kruger, confessed to her best friend that he had throttled Ria. On 5 June 1999, she was sentenced to two years' imprisonment for helping her son tamper with the crime scene to make it look as if her daughter-in-law had been sexually assaulted by an intruder.

Psychopaths go to extreme lengths to get what they want and medical psychopaths are no different. Consequently, there is a high rate of uxorious murder. Dr Bouwer could simply have left his hapless wife for the unwitting new mistress, but instead chose a strange method of poisoning that led to his downfall. Bouwer's searing over-confidence, coupled with contempt for the abilities of those who investigated him, made his conviction a near-certainty. Hubris indeed, but it did not arise out of nowhere and it must be strongly suspected that Bouwer, who had a track record of patient abuse and narcotics dispensing, had engaged in previous try-outs to provide him with encouragement and incentive.

Would Bouwer have gone on to further killing if he had got away with the murder of his wife Annette? It is quite possible. All his life, Bouwer displayed a pattern of ruthless, fraudulent and deceptive behaviour to suit his own ends. He was amoral and unhampered by any ethical restraints. He was intelligent enough to get through medicine and psychiatry and able to sell himself to just about anyone. Once he was exposed, it all fell away, leaving nothing but lies, deception and contempt for anyone who stood in his path.

10

Surgeons, sick and sinister

Surgeons must be very careful
When they take the knife!
Underneath their fine incisions
Stirs the Culprit—Life!

Emily Dickinson, *Complete Poems* (1904)

While the concept of a doctor deliberately killing patients is difficult to accept, both in the public and the professional mind, there is a wider recognition of the clinical chaos, including unnecessary deaths, that can follow when a doctor is obviously unwell but refuses to stop practising. Like a leader in the seat of power, they cannot be deterred or persuaded to step down until it is too late. This results in any number of unnecessary deaths, and enormous distress to their survivors.

The rise of surgery in the second half of the nineteenth century followed the development of aseptic surgery and the use of anaesthesia. This propelled surgeons from the low-status descendants of 'barbers' and bonesetters to equal competitors with physicians. Once medical practice and training was regulated, medicine and surgery soon made a mutually beneficial marriage of convenience, becoming official heirs to the powerful profession that assumed the mantle of medical authority. The apothecaries were the losers in the struggle and survived in the lower status role of pharmacists.

Surgeons were the heirs to a class-based culture of ruthless autonomy, action-based intervention and authoritarian inter-actions with other health care staff and patients. Technical skill is the supreme requirement of the surgeon; any sensible patient will prefer an indifferent, if not rude, master craftsman to a kindly or amiable bumbler. There are many reasons for choosing medicine as a career and manual dexterity is seldom a factor for getting into medical school. The surgeon was seen as a godlike figure, applauded for his efforts in saving lives, not for making mistakes. Patients in turn were expected to be grateful, not complain about the way they had been treated.

The 'Medical Duckshoot Story' illustrates the old attitude of surgeons and the difference between the disciplines: a duck flies overhead; the physician asks whether it is a duck or not, and debates whether tests should be ordered; the duck flies past. When the next duck flies over, the psychiatrist wonders what factors in his upbringing led him to think it is a duck; the duck flies past. Another duck flies over, the surgeon shoots it down and asks, 'What was that?'

By the middle of the twentieth century, the era of the general surgeon was ending. A doctor who had the manual skills for reconstructing the human body, combined with an ability to command and dominate, if not win, the admiration of those around them, was no longer needed. Their work could be done in any number of ways by other doctors in a non-invasive fashion using advanced scanning technology, increasingly requiring virtual technology and visio-spacial skills.

Such experts seldom fell into the old artisanal groups and the great surgical colleges began to lose their relevance. 'Surgery' became just another sunset speciality and surgeons another servant of society, responsible to any number of bureaucratic regulators, rather than godlike dispensers of life. Their image took a battering and slumped from hero to villain.

Modern surgeons say they are far removed from the old stereotype. They are super-specialised, highly trained and work in multidisciplinary teams, subject to a Kafkaesque regulatory environment. They go to extraordinary lengths to keep up with new developments and adopt the latest technology. Despite this, there is no evidence that the public is happier with the outcome. There is a belief, encouraged by any number of judges, that surgery will deliver perfect results every time under any circumstances.

Surgical scandals continue to erupt. For the rest of the profession they are like the canary in the miner's cage, the harbinger of a problem waiting to explode, engulfing everyone. These scandals embody not just the dilemma of the surgeon's craft but all the problems of the modern medical enterprise, providing high-level and faultless care for a gigantic aging population with chronic diseases. With the exception of the rare killers, there will always be surgical scapegoats who, in the majority of cases, are foot-soldier casualties of the high price paid to practise medicine, each infraction magnified by the media, the root cause never examined.

Such doctors may suffer from a neurological or psychiatric condition, drug addiction or alcoholism. Medical regulators have a much higher threshold of awareness of these problems now and are likely to intervene sooner. However, just like telling a superior officer they are unfit to lead, it can be extremely challenging to deter such doctors, and their continued progress may be facilitated by people around them.

Dr Ferdinand Sauerbruch's story illustrates the difficulties when a famous doctor becomes seriously ill, and how this is exploited by the authorities when it suits them. Sauerbruch is one of the most famous surgeons of the twentieth century. He designed a chamber for open-chest surgery in 1904, permitting procedures on the lungs, heart and oesophagus. He developed the radical strategy of rehearsing difficult operations, drilling his team with military precision. He devised several surgical implements and prostheses during World War I. His mentor was the great German surgeon Johann Mikulicz-Rodecki. In an ominous portent, Sauerbruch witnessed Mikulicz's demise, from lapses of skill and mental confusion to strange behaviour before his death from cancer.

Sauerbruch was a mercurial personality, prone to the anger and intolerance of failure associated with an indomitable drive. His unshakable confidence in his own ability produced both good and bad behaviour. He cheated shamelessly in his early examinations. He had no hesitation in telling the rich and famous his opinion, regardless of the effect. In the operating theatre, Sauerbruch was abusive and intolerant; his staff dreaded outbursts when he would lash out while clutching a scalpel. At the same time, Sauerbruch was admired by his staff for his dedication to his patients at all times, and for producing outstanding results. He was disinterested in class where illness was concerned, waiving his fees when operating on the poor.

Away from work, Sauerbruch spent his time chasing women, in nightclubs and restaurants. He drank heavily but it never seemed to affect his operating skills. Such was his fame that he was frequently requested to operate on the rich and famous, including Mussolini, Lenin, General Ludendorff, General Hindenburg and the king of Greece.

When war broke out in 1939, Sauerbruch was head of the Charité Hospital, the most famous in Berlin. During the war, he trained doctors in field surgery and received the Knight's Cross from Hitler. He never made his dislike for Hitler a secret and had a distant connection with the 1944 assassination attempt. However, he escaped any censure. When Berlin fell, Russian soldiers entered the underground bunker theatre where he was operating, but left sheepishly under a hail of abuse from Sauerbruch.

Sauerbruch developed cerebral sclerosis, hardening of the arteries of the brain, now known as vascular or multi-infarct dementia. This led to a catastrophic loss of judgement, outbursts of violent rage and uninhibited, impulsive behaviour.

At the age of 74, Sauerbruch was appointed as head of the rebuilt Charité Hospital, located in the communist sector of East Berlin. The communist authorities were delighted to have a medical star of his prestige under their wing. He was allowed to practise, but it soon became apparent that he was a shadow of his former self. He was protected by the Russians, who gave him gifts and ensured his safety.

Sauerbruch appointed surgeon Max Madlener, who had served with the SS, to the hospital. Dr Friedrich Hall, a neurologist and supervisor of medical facilities in East Berlin, came to investigate. Hall noted that Sauerbruch kept losing the thread of the conversation, talking about dead relatives as though they were still alive. A senior surgeon, Dr Karl Stompfe, resigned after being physically assaulted by Sauerbruch when he pointed out that he was operating with dirty hands.

Hall discovered that complaints from Charité staff about Sauerbruch's decline had been suppressed by senior medical authorities because he was their biggest magnet for donations and fundraising.

Hall confronted Sauerbruch. Sauerbruch's assistant came into the room to say that a patient's cerebral tumour was exposed to view and that in his opinion the prognosis was bad. Sauerbruch leapt to his feet and rushed to the theatre. Within minutes he returned, waving a bloody mass of tissue in his fist, saying to the horrified Hall: 'Look! They think they are surgeons! I went right in and pulled it out. The finger is still the surgeon's best instrument.' The patient died two days later.

In April 1949, Sauerbruch was summoned to a de-Nazification hearing. Defending his award from Hitler, he said, 'I accepted it for all German doctors. It was given to me because I did my duty as a physician.' He delivered a rambling three-hour rant before storming out. Such was the power of the Sauerbruch name that he was exonerated. Still in demand for private consultations as normal life resumed in Europe, Sauerbruch would get lost and wander around airport terminals in confusion.

Hall spoke to Dr Josef Naas, the communist director of the Academy of Sciences in East Berlin. Indifferent to the casualties, Naas refused to bar Sauerbruch from surgery, saying, 'In the coming struggle of the proletariat, millions will lose their lives. It is trivial whether Sauerbruch kills a few dozen people on his operating table. We need the name of Sauerbruch.'

Sauerbruch's behaviour worsened. His staff attempted to shield patients from him, to little effect. During a splenectomy, he tore the organ badly; after removal of a cancer in a boy's stomach, he forgot to re-attach the intestine before closing up; he bungled the removal of a gastric tumour.

Hall confronted Madlener, but his loyalty to Sauerbruch was such that he could not contemplate usurping his master. Finally, when the Charité faced suits for medical negligence, Sauerbruch was forced to retire, leaving only with the greatest reluctance in November 1949.

Patients continued to flock to Sauerbruch's home on Hertatstrasse where Sauerbruch performed operations without anaesthetic on the dining table in his sitting room. He did not sterilise his old instruments and sewed up afterwards with needle and thread from his wife's sewing basket.

By the summer of 1950, neighbours complained about the terrible screams coming from the house. The Board of Health warned Sauerbruch to desist but he ignored them. In desperation, his wife took to waylaying prospective patients, but they would get around her and insist the great doctor operate. She even disconnected the doorbell, but Sauerbruch would find them on his doorstep and invariably invite them in. As she had to go to work to support them, there were plenty of opportunities for him to continue his ways.

Sauerbruch's last patient was Frau Irmgard Liebig (41) who had throat cancer. She recalled his kindness towards her years earlier when Sauerbruch had removed a cancerous breast. Her faith in him was so strong that she silently endured an operation on her throat without anaesthetic. Sauerbruch's wife was so horrified she contacted the medical authorities to intervene. Frau Liebig lingered in agony for months until her death.

Sauerbruch eventually died in August 1951 of a cerebral haemorrhage. It is said that as he sank away, his fingers moved along the edge of the blanket as though he was stitching an incision.

Sauerbruch had a fiery personality and drank heavily. None of this affected his superb surgical skills until he developed vascular dementia. Then, what had been merely tolerable aberrations became all-encompassing, with complete loss of judgement. At first his status as a surgical pioneer was sufficient to intimidate both Nazi and communist authorities to overlook the decline in his hitherto superb surgical skills. By the time action was taken, his work had degenerated into what can only be described as demented hacking and it was too late for his unfortunate victims.

Another surgeon who could easily match Sauerbruch in fame, although not in skill, was Dr John Hamilton Bailey[1]. Bailey was known in every corner of the world where surgery was practised through his textbooks, especially *Demonstration of Physical Signs in Surgery*, the first edition published in 1927 and still in print today. *A Short Practice of Surgery* is the most widely sold book on surgery. Another book, *Emergency Surgery*, has saved countless lives, used by doctors around the world in a variety of isolated or emergency situations, often having someone turn the pages for them as they operate. The books are lavishly illustrated with photographs and drawings, many done by Bailey himself.

John Hamilton Bailey was born at Bishopstoke in October 1894. His father a doctor, Bailey came from a middle-class background and went to a good school. Good at sport, he easily met the requirements to be accepted into medical school, where he excelled but was regarded by his fellows as somewhat remote and unsociable. One of his mentors was Sir Frederick Treves, a brilliant surgeon and humanist, best known for his rescue of the man known as the 'Elephant Man'. In the early years of his training, Bailey had his left index finger amputated following an infection but this never interfered with his career.

It would be expected that successful books on surgery would be written by a leading academic in a prestigious hospital, but this was far from the case. Bailey's rise to consultant surgeon was rapid, his experience facilitated by work as a medical officer during World War I, including service in the Battle of Jutland. Despite his academic ability, experience and teaching skills, Bailey was a difficult character, prone to antagonising colleagues and administrators alike. He moved around various provincial hospitals before ending up at the Royal Northern Hospital, where he spent the last twenty years of his career.

Bailey was obsessed with his work, constantly operating and taking off little time for a social life, although he reluctantly invited referring doctors to his home to ensure a regular flow of patients. He had little interest in money, treating public and private patients alike and never chasing up unpaid debts.

From an early stage in his career, Bailey's surgical work raised questions. He preferred work that required rapid intervention, hence his preference for emergency surgery. But even with routine procedures he had a high death rate. Much of this was attributed to the limited understanding of fluid and electrolyte balance, transfusion reactions and other aspects of post-operative management at the time. It was also a time when the consultant or honorary surgeon was seen as a god, operating on public patients for free. Patients in turn were expected to be grateful for help, not complain about the way they had been treated.

Adrian Marston, Bailey's biographer, commenting on a photograph of him operating, said the table was 'a mess' with far too many bloody swabs and instruments visible. Bailey's technique was characterised by speed, not skill, and his wide sweeps could cause any amount of unnecessary damage.

Bailey's technical skill, Marston says, was 'unfavourable'. He had the diagnostic ability, decisiveness, organisational talent and capacity to know when not to operate but lacked the manual skills essential for operating. However, in those times, the idea of selecting a doctor for surgical training on this basis was not done. Surgeons were applauded for their efforts in attempting to save lives, not criticised for repeated mistakes.

A tragic example of Bailey's detached hauteur occurred after his only son died in a hideous train accident. Returning from school on the train, Hamilton Bailey junior was looking out the window when he was hit by the swinging door of a passing train, almost decapitating him. Bailey was informed of the news in the middle of a gall bladder dissection which he completed, continuing with another operation without comment. The patient later died, her death attributed to a transfusion reaction. But it is difficult to believe that her surgeon did not share some responsibility for continuing to operate in such a distraught, emotional state.

Bailey's work continued to deteriorate. His usual detachment waned, and he became aggressive, moody and erratic. He missed appointments, left a cotton pack in an abdomen and had outbursts of rage at staff. The casualties escalated. Initially, no one considered asking him to cease; in those days, the idea of reporting a surgeon was scarcely thought of. But he could not continue: he could not even do the most simple procedures. The situation became untenable and, after several admissions to psychiatric hospitals or nursing homes, he gave up surgery.

The basis for Bailey's problems was evident. He had manic depression, or bipolar disorder as it is now known. The condition ran in the family. His mother, a fragile personality, was depressed for many years and his only sister was incarcerated from an early age and subjected to a lobotomy for what was then thought to be schizophrenia. In 1949, Bailey was given the new anti-manic treatment of lithium and showed an almost immediate improvement. However, the medication was stopped for reasons that are not clear and he slowly deteriorated.

Bailey and his wife spent the last years of his life in Málaga, Spain. By then he probably had brain damage from the treatments he had been subjected to, including unmodified ECT and insulin coma therapy. Nevertheless, he continued working on his books until the end.

Bailey's demise was a reprise of a situation that had occurred with many of his patients. He developed a cancer of the colon. It was in the early stages and a colostomy, followed by a routine removal would have led to a complete cure. However, unable to the last to change his ways, Bailey interfered, insisting that the surgeon do a complicated and quite unnecessary colectomy. He developed post-operative infection and died of peritonitis, adding himself to the long list of surgical tragedies that had arisen from his elevated sense of his own value, and inability to accept that he could be wrong, or consider the sentient nature of his patients.

Hamilton Bailey had everything a surgeon needs—but the essential manual skills. His mood, attitude and behaviour were driven by his bipolar disorder—chiefly mania—making his judgement even more suspect.

11

The deepest sleep

Dr Harry Bailey and the deepest sleep of all

I wondered how anyone could ever imagine unquiet slumbers for the sleepers in that quiet earth.

Emily Bronte, *Wuthering Heights*

A patient is ushered into a consulting room in Macquarie Street, Sydney's equivalent to Harley Street. The room is large, in contrast to the shoeboxes used by most specialists, and stocked with antique furniture. It is surprisingly dark. The door closes behind her. The doctor sits in a circle of light at the large desk. He indicates, with a jerk of his head, for her to sit down. He has a large shock of hair, now turning grey. The face, once handsome and suave, is crumbling from years of hard living.

On the desk, a human brain sits in a pathology bottle, bobbing gently in a sea of formalin, small vessels and strips of membrane dangling from the gelid organ like fronds of seaweed in the slowly discolouring fluid. Through an open door at the back is a storeroom resembling a pharmacy with shelves full of psychotropic drugs with names like Parstelin and Neulactil.

The doctor fixes the patient with a stare, long enough to intimidate her. He listens to her story, from time to time inclining his head to the side and nodding to encourage her. The patient, a young attractive woman, finishes. There is a pause. Then the doctor leans forward, his eyebrows slightly lifted and, with what looks like a gleam in his eyes, says, 'What you need is a good fuck.'

The inability to admit one can be wrong exemplifies the ancient Greek sin of hubris. This explains the most puzzling aspect of clinicide: the doctor who cannot step back from the casualties of treatment at an early stage and seek assistance or give up what they are doing. From Shipman and Adams to Hamilton Bailey there was a fatal hubris, permitting these doctors to perceive themselves as supremely dedicated, if not heroic, and any criticism of or intervention in their work was responded to in paranoid terms. One of the worst examples is described here.

Heading the list of clinicidal doctors in Australia is Sydney psychiatrist Dr Harry Bailey who was responsible for the Chelmsford deep-sleep scandal. From 1963 to 1978, large numbers of patients were treated by a dubious treatment modality, deep-sleep therapy (DST), in a Sydney suburban cottage hospital. On the slimmest of pretexts, patients were put into deep levels of coma with high doses of drugs under minimum supervision or care. By the time it was investigated,

Bailey was found to be responsible for at least 87 deaths and several hundred casualties.

The perpetrator of this appalling abuse of psychiatric treatment was Dr Harry Richard Bailey. Born at Picton, New South Wales, to a working-class family in 1922, Bailey was sent to boarding school to help him fulfil early academic promise. He was a largely unremarked-upon figure at medical school, despite winning final-year prizes for paediatrics and psychiatry (coming first in the latter out of a field of three entrants). By the time he graduated, Bailey had married. He went on to qualify in the largely disdained field of psychiatry, seeing in this opportunities for self-advancement that would not be available in other, more conventional, specialist disciplines.

The first indication of Bailey's opportunism was winning a World Health Organisation scholarship. The scholarship was intended to provide him with the opportunity to investigate overseas psychiatric treatment. This was a rarely awarded bursary and it remains a mystery how Bailey, who had never done research, managed to snare such a prize.

After visiting psychiatric centres around the world, including the prestigious Karolinska Institute in Sweden, Bailey returned to Sydney after eighteen months. His visits were brief and he was little more than a passing visitor at any of these centres. However, among his contacts was a meeting with the notorious Dr Ewan Cameron of Toronto, who was involved in experiments for a CIA-directed 'mind control' program, as well as in high-voltage electro-convulsive therapy trials.

It did not take long before Bailey, an assiduous self-promoter, was engaging in showmanship.

'Human Guinea Pigs in Test', said the headline in a Sydney paper in September 1957. 'A Sydney mental health specialist and 15 other volunteers deliberately sent themselves temporarily insane in recent mental research tests.' Bailey and some colleagues had taken mescaline and LSD to raise hope for 'mental cases'. He described his trip: 'You look at the light and it turns into a palm tree. The drab walls of a room glow with beautiful colours.' 'By these experiments', the paper stated, 'he hopes to trace the section of the brain affected by schizophrenia'.

Claiming to be a world authority, Bailey told the Sydney media that new surgical techniques were available to cure previously intractable psychiatric conditions. In 1957 Bailey persuaded the NSW government to establish the Cerebral Surgery Unit (CSU), promising a world-class psychosurgery centre to cure mental patients. Seduced by his claim to empty the psychiatric hospitals, the politicians provided Bailey with the then huge sum of one million pounds for his project. That it was already recognised that psychosurgery had a limited future did not deter Bailey, who was getting a reputation as something of a miracle-maker, if not a psychiatric showman.

The CSU was typical of Bailey's grandiose world view. An elaborate complex was established and staffed. No expense was spared in getting the latest neurosurgical equipment. Bailey had a large office with an electronic door that was opened and closed with a button under his desk. Indicating that his grandiosity was accompanied by a degree of paranoia, a secret voice-operated recording system was installed in the office so he could listen to conversations in other rooms through the intercom.

Callan Park Hospital (later known as Rozelle Hospital), where the unit was established, was the largest psychiatric hospital in Australia. Capitalising on his prestige, Bailey was appointed superintendent, presumably seeing the position as an extension of his power. However, he soon became disillusioned: treating severely disturbed patients in a sprawling asylum held little appeal. In addition, the glamour associated with the CSU faded. Despite all the hoopla, they never did much more than routine psychosurgery operations. His chiliastic promises notwithstanding, it was clear the psychiatric wards were not going to empty and Bailey soon tired of supervising a large team of neurosurgeons, neurologists and other workers. His response—possibly in anticipation of the inevitable questions about justifying the cost of the CSU—was to leak information to the press about alleged corruption and mismanagement in the hospital. Needless to say, in these accounts Bailey portrayed himself as a heroic fighter against corruption.

His attempts to attack the state government backfired and a Royal Commission was appointed. The recommendations led to him being fired; his career in the public sector ended under controversial circumstances. Undeterred, Bailey went into private practice in 1963, determined that he would not be beholden to bureaucratic control in carrying out his plans. He set up rooms in Macquarie Street, promoting himself as a psychiatric authority to both doctors and the public.

Bailey saw private practice as a competitive business, unlike his conservative colleagues who frowned on anything that could be regarded as advertising or self-promotion. He had an electric typewriter fitted with a green ink ribbon, made a point of using expensive stationery with waxed print that stood out, and put distinctive first-day-of-issue stamps on his envelopes. He insisted on signing letters and cheques in green ink, telling a colleague that it would make people remember him.

Bailey became an honorary physician to the Crown Street Women's Hospital, where his obsession with sexuality led to the establishment of a Department of Gynaecological Psychiatry.

He used a series of slides with drawings of sexual positions to teach medical students and, showing the utter insensitivity to patients that characterised his work, would sometimes insist on getting female patients to demonstrate how to masturbate in front of a group of medical students. To the relief of many, he left the hospital after a few years.

It is at this point that the public Bailey was established. Able to discuss any psychiatric problem in a convincing manner, he was the image of a mind doctor, a modern Freud. Tall, dark and handsome with a penetrating gaze, dressed in good suits, he was described as intense, saturnine and riveting. He cultivated doctors and lawyers; before long he was telling judges he could cure convicted criminals of behavioural problems ranging from drug addiction to homosexuality. As a result, he had no difficulty instituting a lucrative practice. The money rolled in, facilitated by his penchant for charging high fees and constantly making fraudulent Medicare and private insurance claims. Bailey drove the latest model imported car and lived the high life, cultivating an image as a bon vivant with a circle of friends. They would go out for meals, attend the opera and drink the finest wines.

Gynaecologist Jules Black, who knew Bailey at Crown Street Women's Hospital, witnessed his inappropriate social life and behaviour. Wanting a backyard pool at his house in Haberfield, not prepared to wait for council permission, he simply dynamited a hole, fracturing the main sewer pipe for the whole street. Invited to a meal at the Bailey home, Jules Black found an impeccable table groaning with magnificent crockery and cutlery, superb food and the highest quality wine. Yet they were met at the door by Bailey wearing Bermuda shorts and a florid Hawaiian shirt with a monocle set in his eye—a surprising presentation for a high-flyer. A room in the home had a plaque on the door that read 'Neurosurgical Research Laboratory' for tax purposes. Bailey gleefully demonstrated his enormous collection of medieval maces, spears and clubs.

Accompanying the flamboyant hedonism was Bailey's rampant promiscuity, at times amounting to satyriasis. Adultery with nurses, wives and secretaries did not satisfy; he was a regular predator on patients. His approach was less than subtle. Without any ado, he would say to a female patient, 'What you need is a good fuck', and offer to remedy this deficit immediately. His success with this approach varied, depending on the gullibility or vulnerability of the patient involved, but he had a number of long-term affairs with disturbed women whom he continued to treat, unconcerned about the inappropriate situation he had created. It was one of these affairs—with Sharon Hamilton—that haunted him until the end of his days.

Once he went into private practice, Bailey remained preoccupied with his grand vision of a biological treatment of all psychiatric illnesses. He continued to refer patients for psychosurgery, but it was becoming clear this had limited application in severe cases of depression and obsessive-compulsive disorder. While a compliant neurosurgeon was available to do the operations, there was a growing public disquiet about the surgery. Bailey decided to follow a different path, one that could be offered to a far greater range of patients, was easier to apply and would remain under his complete control: deep-sleep therapy (DST).

DST has a long history in psychiatry. Since time immemorial the idea that sleep would soothe the savage breast, as it were, had resonated with psychiatrists; if you could be induced to sleep during a violent emotional crisis, then all would be well when you woke up. For several centuries the only available psychiatric drugs—alcohol and opiates—did little else but make patients sleep. However, with the development of more sophisticated drugs like barbiturates, putting a patient into a prolonged state of sleep became a possibility. There was little scientific work done to investigate its efficacy and DST was seldom, if ever, used in public or teaching hospitals, but only by individual practitioners. The main proponent of DST was flamboyant English psychiatrist Dr William Sargant, and it appears he and Bailey kept in some contact over the years.

In 1963, after a trial run at one hospital had to be abandoned because the matron disapproved, Bailey set up a DST ward in the small cottage hospital known as Chelmsford in Pennant Hills, Sydney. He soon found several doctors who came under his sway, and were happy to assist and never question DST.

The DST process at Chelmsford Hospital resembled a medical hijacking rather than a voluntary admission for psychiatric care. When patients came to the waiting room, they filled out the admission sheet and were handed several tablets to swallow. If they asked, they were told this was routine practice. In most cases, this was the last thing the patients remembered. They would become extremely drowsy, if not comatose, and were taken to the bed where they were regularly dosed with a fantastic combination of barbiturates, sedatives and antipsychotic drugs. If it was decided that electro-convulsive therapy (ECT) was to be used, it was given while they were in bed without the drugs used to minimise side effects: because of the fit induced by the electric current, a short-acting anaesthetic (such as pentothal) is usually used, followed by a muscle relaxant, such as scoline, to prevent injuries such as broken teeth, bitten tongues or torn muscles.

As DST was already a treatment of dubious value when Bailey started using it, Sargant insisted that patients needed intensive monitoring and skilled care. Guidelines included making sure the patient was able to walk, could be easily woken up and that treatment was stopped immediately if complications set in. Bailey did no more than insist that untrained and unsupervised nurses—there were usually six patients to one nurse—use the maximum doses of sedative drugs to attain the deepest comas. Patients were not even seen by a doctor on admission; their prescriptions were typed out in advance.

Left alone for lengthy periods, lying on their backs with impaired respiration from excessive sedation—a characteristic of barbiturate overdose—patients choked on their own vomit and went into cardio-respiratory collapse. Thrombosis, pneumonia, peritonitis, strokes, heart attacks, and brain damage were typical results. For many, living with the consequences of DST, there was only one way out—suicide.

Dying or dead patients were put in an ambulance and sent to nearby Hornsby Hospital, where casualty staff became almost inured to seeing them. As casualties mounted and the body count rose, Bailey made no attempt to improve the procedure or provide better care and supervision. If moribund patients could not be taken away, the death certificate gave an anodyne explanation of cardiac or respiratory failure as the cause of death. To maintain the cover-up, forms were frequently altered after death to indicate that there had been another illness present. Bailey's dishonesty was meretricious and all-encompassing. He would lie or falsify facts under any circumstances to suit himself, on some occasions giving blatantly false evidence in court. He seemed quite undeterred by this, insisting to people around him that he was being unjustly victimised for his pioneering and dedicated work.

Bailey's undoing started with his affair with Sharon Hamilton. She was a young dancer who was attacked by a prisoner during a performance at a local jail. Bailey took her on as a patient and gave testimony in court that ensured she got an insurance payment of $100,000, a very large sum at the time. Hamilton was soon addicted to both prescription drugs and Bailey. A series of suicide bids followed; he would admit her to the hospital, and come round to her private room to dally with her. However, as she plunged deeper into depression and drug dependence, she could not relinquish her attachment to Bailey even though at some level she recognised how destructive the situation was. A series of arguments and reconciliations followed. Bailey admitted to friends he was finding her a bother and had to bring the affair to an end.

Sharon Hamilton eventually died of a drug overdose in her flat under mysterious circumstances. Bailey, who inherited her estate, was the central figure in the two coronial inquiries that followed, and he was fortunate to escape prosecution. However, under the strain of the inquiries, he became depressed, no surprise considering how his life was unravelling. His DST cases were being taken to court, he had left his wife and moved in with his secretary, and was hitting the bottle.

His mood slumped, he became suicidal and was given a knock-out injection by his chief assistant, Dr John Herron, in much the same way the unwitting patients were gulled on arrival at Chelmsford Hospital. In a poignant irony, Bailey was admitted anonymously to his own ward under the name Harry Lee and given DST. The only concession to his status was that Herron kept the coma as light as possible and carefully monitored his progress, a luxury denied the other patients. After he came out of the coma, Bailey never learned that he had undergone DST, believing he was given ECT and had lost memory of the time.

Bailey appeared to recover from his depression, but was never again as ebullient. His patients at the hospital could often wait all day to see him without success. He would turn up after midnight, mostly the worse from drink, and make an impromptu ward round, paying little attention to concerns raised by the staff, but always ensuring the patients were later billed. Despite the problems, DST at Chelmsford Hospital continued without restraint, only stopping in 1979 when psychiatrists refused to admit their patients. Being a private hospital, the owners were largely dependent on a regular supply of patients referred by the psychiatrists for their income. As a result, Bailey was asked to leave, providing a weird example of the benefits of free-market medical economics.

Bailey's problems escalated and it became evident that a long struggle lay ahead with only one possible outcome for him. The actions of patients such as Barry Hart, who had a long and discouraging struggle to get justice, along with persistent media reports, kept the issue in the public domain and eventually brought Bailey to face the courts. As his problems mounted, his paranoia mounted.

The publicity, investigations and court cases continued without avail. Bailey presented a miserable figure in court, using legal technicalities to avoid or defer cases, sneezing continuously from some allergy, and was hounded by the press or anti-psychiatry activists when he ventured outside.

When his insurance company refused liability for further defence costs in September 1985, Bailey snapped, walking out of the meeting. He was found dead in his car near Gosford, having taken an overdose of sleeping tablets washed down with a German beer. He wrote a trite suicide note, illustrated with a poem, lashing out at his persecutors and portraying himself as a pioneering martyr to scientific progress. Too dejected by then to care, Bailey did not note the final irony: the Tuinal with which he killed himself was the mainstay of DST, a sleep from which many victims never awoke.

There is one record of Bailey's attempts to justify his treatment. A recording was made of a talk he gave to the nurses at Chelmsford. In a rambling, even wild, monologue he drifted across the neuroscience of psychosurgery, dredging up old research and conjuring up wacky explanations for psychiatric conditions, in the process becoming crude and incoherent:

When I was working in America in New Orleans, there was experimental work being done there on cats, where they found that if you put electrodes down on the anterior part of the brain, in the septal region between the two hemispheres and down, right deep down, sort of here, put electrodes in here, that you struck a [inaudible] which had something to do with screwing and orgasm and pleasure and satisfaction.

And if they put a wire in this and took it out and put it on to a push button, the cat would very quickly know that if it pressed the button, it got a little 'chop', and this was a sort of a little orgasm. And so the cat would go 'pop' again, and get the taste of it, and the cat would go 'pop, pop, pop, pop'. Here was something important. What did you make of it?

This was the carrot in front of the animal's nose, you see. If you didn't have orgasms, nobody would screw. But if you have orgasms, this works like a carrot in front of everybody's nose—'Wow, wasn't that a beaut?'

And therefore if you're screwing and you have an orgasm, it lasts for ten years. Boy, this is good value for money! And these kids, you see, they never had it so good, they load themselves up on their pot and screw the backsides off each other as long as they can. And that's why you've got to stamp out pot, that's why. That's the problem, because... is a substance which damages DNA...

I have a theory which I'm only saying inside this room—it is completely unfounded, but I've got a theory that the reason why all these viruses are eating us up alive [inaudible]—the viruses are chopping us to pieces—it's because these viruses are passing through all these pot smokers and developing greater malignity, simply because the pot smokers have got very little immunity left. Now, that's a crazy theory, but anyhow maybe in ten years' time...

The Bailey of old—articulate, convincing, authoritative—was long gone; by then he was reduced to a shadow, a bloated alcoholic stripped of all charm, sitting in the dark in an empty consulting room, staring at the preserved brain floating in a bottle on his desk.

Following further media revelations, in 1988 the Slattery Royal Commission conducted a detailed review of Bailey's practice, making him in the process the only man in Australian history to have two Royal Commissions inquiring into his activities. The finding was that at least 87 patients had died, and many more had been seriously affected by physical and psychiatric consequences, from treatment with DST.

The full extent of the tragedy will never be known. There were 22 suicides of DST patients. Some victims were horrified to find out what had been done to them only when they were eventually before the Royal Commission to give testimony.

DST was banned as a treatment in New South Wales and a new system of medical regulation and discipline was set up to investigate erring doctors. The Royal Commission also gave some insight into the role of system factors in allowing DST to continue. The Royal Australian and New Zealand College of Psychiatrists had no powers to discipline, let alone expel, wayward members. The rest of the medical profession shrugged off the situation or adopted the view that psychiatry was, in any event, too far out of the zone of 'real medicine' to matter.

There seemed to be a pattern of incompetence, waywardness or corruption extending to the highest level in the NSW Health Commission in dealing with the situation. When Health Department officials came to Chelmsford Hospital, they were more interested in details such as the measurement of the doorways, rather than what was occurring in a darkened ward with moaning, incontinent patients sliding into moribund somnolence. Whether Bailey had some political sway or a 'godfather' protecting him will never be known, but the institutional system can only be described as passively, or perhaps even actively, facilitating his activities.

Bailey worked with three other doctors at Chelmsford. One was a senior psychiatrist who described Bailey's methods as merely misunderstood, if occasionally excessive. Another, who came regularly to the hospital to give ECT, was professionally obscure and seemed grateful to have the job without any need to inquire deeper. The third had a financial interest in the hospital, benefiting from the admissions. Between them they seemed to exemplify the motives of doctors who become partners, associates or facilitators of clinicide.

There have been many attempts to understand Bailey and his motives. It was a time when psychiatric illness was little understood and widely feared. There is no disputing that Bailey was a charismatic figure who convinced politicians, judges, doctors and many others. The imposing figure of a confident doctor who offered a magical cure for otherwise hopeless situations, bolstered by what was claimed to be a distinguished record of study and research, was difficult to resist.

Bailey was described by the Royal Commissioner, Justice Slattery, as 'two-faced, devious, dissembling and unprincipled, subject to severe mood swings... (with) a tendency to be flamboyant, to exaggerate, to shock'. Bailey's dishonesty was extreme and psychopathic, putting him squarely in the zone in which the worst medical killers operated. He had no hesitation in sexually abusing vulnerable patients, cheating on fees or conniving to hide evidence.

Professional anti-psychiatrist Thomas Szasz said that 'Bailey did what he did because he was an evil, sadistic killer. The fact that he was intelligent and had impressive medical credentials has no bearing on his being evil—Robespierre, Stalin, Hitler, etc. were also no dummies. On the contrary, all that, plus the psychiatric Zeitgeist (spirit of the age), made it easier for him to disguise his brutalities as medical treatment.'

Bailey spent his money on cars, wine and food. He had intense mood swings associated with the midnight ward rounds. He was sexually promiscuous, disinhibited and impulsive. In addition to the constant crude sexual importuning of female patients, he was prone to eccentric, inappropriate or odd remarks, telling one young man that he divided everyone into Martians and Earthlings. There is abundant evidence of grandiose, if not paranoid, thinking. These are typical features of manic depression.

Bailey's unusual behaviour may have resulted from neurological damage. A bad attack of mumps when he was young caused sterility. He had at least one episode of pneumonia and a severe attack of hepatitis in 1975. The intriguing possibility is that these infectious illnesses could have led to encephalitis causing personality changes. This phenomenon was first documented after the 1919 influenza epidemic, which caused brain disease with features of Parkinson's disease in survivors. The encephalitis was associated with personality changes, mood swings, anger and loss of control of moral behaviour.[1] Could this explain why a promising and idealistic young clinician deviated so far from the goals and ideals of his profession?

A comparison can be made between Shipman and Bailey. Like Shipman, Bailey also came from humble origins, was a clever student and made an early marriage at medical school to a partner who seemed notably different in character. Academic and professional ability, a convincing image of professional skill and dedication, overweening egotism combined with an elitist arrogance, indifference to human emotion and utter contempt for their victims are other commonalities with Shipman. The paths diverge after that, Bailey going on to public recognition as a prominent psychiatrist and running the DST program. Effusive, sociable, promiscuous, manipulative, alcoholic and manic depressive, Bailey would seem to be a very different personality from the softly spoken Shipman.

Manic depression notwithstanding, Bailey remains an enigma. At some level he believed deeply that he was offering a unique treatment for mental illness and it was only the means that were problematic. In this, he went beyond charismatic and grandiose to deluded. Yet Bailey killed his patients with abandon. While the first deaths may have been rationalised as unfortunate consequences of treatment, it would have been impossible to maintain this belief as the bodies piled up. As the death count rose, this rationalisation would have become untenable, and some nexus in the mind of the doctor administering treatment and the death of the hapless patients would have been impossible to ignore. This was clinicide of an extraordinary degree, and Bailey remains Australia's worst medical serial killer.

12

Killing with kindness

When euthanasia falls into the hands of the charismatic doctor

Our medical men exert their utmost skill to save the life of every one to the last moment... Thus the weak members of civilised societies propagate their kind. No one who has attended to the breeding of domestic animals will doubt that this must be highly injurious to the race of man.

Charles Darwin, *The Descent of Man*

Euthanasia is the ultimate ethical issue in medical practice. In a profession mandated to save life, no other issue generates such intensity and approbation. And, as shown, it spills right across the territory in which serial, treatment and political medical killers operate. CASK killers[1]—as in carer-assisted serial killing—and serial killers like Shipman use euthanasia as a defence, capitalising on widespread acceptance of the doctor's role in ameliorating painful death. This argument may have worked for Adams, but defendants have had mixed results since then.

Euthanasia is the act of killing or permitting the death of hopelessly sick or injured individuals in a relatively painless way for reasons of mercy. The medical role is to deny, defer or, when demise is inevitable, make death as painless as possible. Euthanasia has a long history but only became an issue in the nineteenth century with the development of high-potency drugs administered by syringe. It did not take long for both doctor and patient to realise that when a horrible, if not protracted, death lay ahead, a swift and painless exit could be induced through a needle.

To illustrate the issues this can expose, it is worth examining a historical case that reveals that even a monarch, in full view of his family, if not the nation, can fall victim to euthanasia by a clinicidal doctor. The case is that of King George V at the hands of his physician, Lord Dawson of Penn.

Lord Dawson of Penn, the royal physician, was the most admired and respected doctor of his generation. He was president of the Royal College of Physicians, twice elected president of the British Medical Association, and honoured with a viscountcy. His treatment of King George V's respiratory illness in 1928 made him a national celebrity.

The last four kings of England all died of smoking-related disease. King George V at age 71 was no exception; he had been in failing health with chronic bronchitis for some months. Accounts of the king's last days by the Archbishop of Canterbury and others tell of tranquil and pain-free afternoons with the king sitting in an armchair before a log fire, becoming gradually weaker. Four days before George V's death, Queen Mary sent for Dawson. The queen and the prince of Wales—who was to become Edward VIII and then the duke of Windsor—told Dawson that they did not want the king's life needlessly prolonged if his illness was fatal. The king was not consulted about this.

On 20 January 1936, the morning of his last day of life, the king managed a ten-minute meeting with his Privy Counsellors. At 9.25 p.m. Dawson issued the medical bulletin that became a classic:

The King's life is moving peacefully toward its close.

The archbishop of Canterbury prayed at the bedside of the semi-comatose king. Dawson, who did not consult the other doctors involved in the king's management, prepared a syringe with three-quarters of a grain of morphine and one grain of cocaine. Sister Catherine Black, the king's nurse, refused to give the lethal injection. Her autobiography in 1939 made no mention of what must have been an extraordinarily difficult situation.

Dawson's diary describes his actions:

At about 11 o'clock it was evident that the last stage might endure for many hours, unknown to the patient but little comporting with the dignity and serenity which he so richly merited and which demanded a brief final scene. Hours of waiting just for the mechanical end when all that is really life has departed only exhausts the onlookers and keeps them so strained that they cannot avail themselves of the solace of thought, communion or prayer. I therefore decided to determine the end and injected (myself) morphia gr.3/4 and shortly afterwards cocaine gr.1 into the distended jugular vein.

Dawson phoned his wife in London to 'advise *The Times* to hold back publication'. The king died within an hour after the injections.

The next morning *The Times* headline read:

A Peaceful Ending at Midnight.

As an example of the sanitisation of history, it was reported that the king's last words were: 'How is the Empire?' But Dawson's notes report a different—and singularly appropriate—response to the doctor hastening his demise. Injected with morphine in the jugular vein, 'God damn you', said the king as he slipped away.

Dawson wanted to ensure that the announcement of the king's death should appear first in the morning edition of *The Times*, rather than 'the less appropriate evening journals'. At the same time, hastening the king's death allowed him to get back to his busy practice in London.

In a House of Lords' debate ten months later, Dawson described euthanasia as a 'mission of mercy', best left to the conscience of individual physicians rather than regulators. He went on, 'If we cannot cure for heaven's sake let us do our best to lighten the pain'.

There is no reason to think that King George V was the only patient Dawson treated in this way. Dawson died in 1945 and his intervention in the reigning monarch's death only came to light 50 years later with the publication of his notes. The emergence of the story did not diminish the stigma which attaches to doctors who take it upon themselves to determine when death shall occur. Despite the presence of two doctors, a nursing sister and the archbishop of Canterbury, Dawson alone assumed the right to determine the circumstances, notably the timing, of the king's death. But most supporters of euthanasia would hesitate to describe the killing of an unconscious patient, without the patient's prior knowledge or consent—let alone their family's—as mercy killing. All too frequently, such cases turn out to be examples not of mercy killing, but convenience, indulgence or narcissistic killing. The person who benefited most from the time of the king's death was Dawson (to say nothing of *The Times*).

The king's death was a mere prelude to what followed. Subverted for racial goals, euthanasia reached its nadir under the Nazis. In October 1939, a month after the invasion of Poland, Hitler ordered 'mercy killing' of the sick and disabled. The Aktion T4 program first killed newborn and very young children with congenital or incurable illnesses, but soon expanded to include older children and adults, notably those with psychiatric illness. An unprecedented genocide followed, administered by the German medical profession, with psychiatrists leading the way. This led inexorably to the gas chambers of Auschwitz.

The Nuremberg Hearings on medical experimentation in 1946 led to an intense debate on how the doctors descended to such depths.[2] Was it the 'bad egg' theory—frustrated or incompetent careerists exploiting the situation for their own ends, or the slippery slope—once a profession had compromised themselves by making the initial concessions, was it a gradual process of degenerating into moral disarray? The consensus was for the slippery slope theory and, chillingly, each case started with the belief that euthanasia could be justified.

After the Nuremberg Hearings, euthanasia went into a recession that turned out to be temporary. In 1957, a trial in an English seaside town with all the set-piece elements of an Agatha Christie thriller, but lacking the expected denouement, provoked a degree of *schadenfreude*. The case involved wealthy old ladies whose death was quickened by injections administered by a mendicant, greedy doctor, Dr Adams.

By the end of the twentieth century, euthanasia had become a cultural, social and medical battleground for a range of competing agendas. The contested terrain extended over the power of the medical profession versus the right of the individual to determine treatment, the reaction to dehumanising high-tech management of severe or chronic illness in impersonal settings away from home and family, loss of confidence in the ability of the medical profession to provide perfect cures, if not defer death, and the rise of anti-scientific beliefs such as communicating with the afterlife.

With the growth of an aging population prone to degenerative illnesses, euthanasia assumed a new mantle. The legalisation movement gained ground with the use of medical technology to prolong the lives of terminal or comatose patients who are unable to communicate their wishes.

It is harder to justify euthanasia now that there is palliative care. This offers a sophisticated multidisciplinary approach, the use of respite care homes, inclusion of the patient and their family in the decision-making process, and expertise in the process of administering drugs to terminal patients.

Most legal systems consider euthanasia to be murder, though in many jurisdictions a physician may lawfully decide not to prolong the patient's life or give drugs to relieve pain even if they shorten the patient's life. In 1997 Oregon became the first state in the United States to decriminalise physician-assisted suicide. Associations promoting legal euthanasia exist in many countries, but euthanasia was only legalised in The Netherlands in 2001 and in Belgium in 2002. It was in this environment that there arose a charismatic doctor who left a trail of bodies in his wake: Jack Kevorkian.

Born on 28 May 1928 in Pontiac, Michigan, Jack Kevorkian's parents escaped the Turkish Genocide of the Armenians in World War I. Kevorkian's constant reiteration of the gory details of the Armenian Genocide indicated his early preoccupation with death. Intelligent, with a bewildering range of interests, but having poor social skills, Kevorkian graduated from the University of Michigan in 1952 and specialised in pathology— the study of tissues, organs and corpses to determine the cause of disease or death. During his internship, he performed an unusual study of dying hospital patients to show the changes in the corneal blood vessels at the moment of death.

Kevorkian served fifteen months as an army medical officer in Korea and returned to pathology. He never did clinical work with patients after this. He broke off an engagement with a store clerk on the grounds that she was not disciplined enough. This left him with plenty of time for writing and playing Bach on a concert organ and a harpsichord.

In the meantime, his study of the history of autopsies continued. In 1958, Kevorkian met death-row convicts at Ohio State Penitentiary to discuss doing medical experiments at their executions to discover new cures. At the time of execution, Kevorkian planned to put the condemned prisoners to sleep with drugs, perform experiments and finally inject lethal drugs.

At Pontiac General hospital, Kevorkian decided to experiment with transfusing blood from corpses. When a victim of a heart attack or car accident was brought in dead on arrival, the team would do a quick autopsy, put the body on a tilt table, stick a needle in the jugular, drain out the blood and give it to a living subject. What the hospital management thought of this is unknown. By then they had adopted the policy that Kevorkian was best ignored as long as the autopsies were performed. The wisdom of this policy, or rather lack thereof, was revealed when Kevorkian came up with a new twist to the experiment: transfusing blood directly from a corpse to an injured soldier during combat. Using himself and staff as subjects, he posed for pictures with the corpses and took the proposal to the US Military, which was less than impressed and dismissed him out of hand. Ironically the experiments resulted in delayed revenge for Kevorkian. He caught hepatitis C from one of the corpses and is now dying of the condition.[3]

Kevorkian's subsequent career was erratic. In 1979, he moved between Michigan and California. He made a movie of Handel's *Messiah* which was never released. In 1983, Kevorkian 'retired' to devote his time to his death-row campaign. His research convinced him that modern methods of execution were inferior to the way it was done in the French Revolution or medieval India.

In a 1968 article in *Medicine and Law*, Kevorkian praised Nazi doctors for trying to get some good out of concentration camp deaths by conducting medical experiments. The Nazis performed 'merciless killing', not mercy killing, he wrote, but 'such horrendous infringement of a concept does not necessarily invalidate it'. Kevorkian felt that a 'good death' did not go far enough and proposed euthanasia with few restrictions. He planned 'obitoria' centres for medically assisted suicide and killing research on consenting adults. Patients who did not wish to be anaesthetised could remain conscious during some experiments.

In his 1991 book *Prescription: Medicide* Kevorkian wrote:

> Lethal injection is probably the most tolerable method on a subjective level. But when it comes to technicalities of performance, the guillotine doubtlessly is easier to use, more uniformly consistent, and absolutely certain. And having an elephant squash the victim's head is the quickest of all...

His goal was to conduct experiments on living people to 'penetrate the mystery of death'. He believed in experimentation on the dying, and death-row organ harvesting. After the execution of Gary Gilmore, Kevorkian wrote to condemned criminals and asked prison authorities to give consent to his proposal. All refused to cooperate.

He developed the concept of *optional assisted suicide* for terminally ill people, those with 'crippling deformities', those suffering from 'intense anxiety or psychic torture', and those seeking suicide as a result of 'religious or philosophical tenets or inflexible personal convictions'. These euthanasia clinics were to be staffed by doctors who would legally terminate people who requested death. While the first 'patients' would be the terminally ill, the clinics would eventually terminate 'patients tortured by other than organic diseases'.

From as early as June 1987, Kevorkian placed classified ads in local papers seeking volunteers but got little response. In the summer of 1989, David Rivlin, a 38-year-old quadriplegic in a nursing home in Detroit, publicly asked him for help. Kevorkian designed the Thanatron machine (Greek for 'death machine') for $30. To avoid legal problems and to minimise coercion, the patient would 'pull the trigger' by pressing a button to start a thiopental drip and set off a 60-second timer. The thiopental would put the patient into a deep coma. After a minute, the timer would send a lethal dose of potassium chloride through the line, stopping the heart in minutes.

Following Rivlin's death, Kevorkian was in business. He adapted the machines, using different chemicals, later carbon monoxide, to leave the responsibility with the patient, rather than the doctor, for initiating the process. Becoming the object of a 1992 Michigan law forbidding such activity, Kevorkian responded that the law denied individuals the right to choose how and when they died. By the time he was jailed in 1998, he had assisted at least 130 people to die.

Kevorkian, who was unregistered as a clinician, paid little attention to the patient's history or clinical symptoms. It was revealed that many of his patients were not terminal; in some cases, the presence of disease was not even verified. Seventy per cent of the nearly 130 people who died in Kevorkian's purpose-built van or at other venues were not terminally ill. Most were disabled and depressed. At least five had no discernible illnesses whatsoever at autopsy. He seemed preoccupied with promoting his own agenda and achieving as much publicity as possible in the process.

In 1991, Marjorie Wantz, his second victim, complained about intractable pelvic pain. However, she was mentally disturbed and the autopsy showed there was no disease.

Sherry Miller, the third assisted suicide, had multiple sclerosis but was upset by her divorce and worried about burdening her parents with her care.

Esther Cohan, age 46, with multiple sclerosis, died in 1995. She arrived in Michigan in a neglected physical state, covered with bed sores, which should have been attended to immediately by any caring physician when he saw her.

Rebecca Badger, age 39, who died in 1996, also believed she had multiple sclerosis. Badger was a depressed alcoholic who was addicted to pain pills. The autopsy revealed that she was not physically ill.

Judith Curren, age 42, was diagnosed with chronic fatigue syndrome, a scarcely lethal condition. She was flown to Kevorkian in 1996. The autopsy detected no disease.

In 1998, quadriplegic Joseph Tushkowski underwent 'bizarre mutilation' after his death. In a scene the medical examiner called out of a 'slaughterhouse', Kevorkian lifted up Tushkowski's sweater, tied off the blood vessels with twine and ripped out the kidneys. At a news conference he offered the organs for transplant, saying: 'First come, first served.'

By now, Kevorkian was making world-wide headlines. Constantly seeking publicity and showing no hesitation in attacking the medical establishment, he had little difficulty in attracting a cohort of followers and admirers, many of whom had widely differing agendas. At a series of trials he managed to escape conviction under the existing laws, causing intense public controversy. Increasingly grandiose, Kevorkian did everything he could to provoke the authorities to charge and try him. He appeared to believe his own publicity, namely that authorities would not dare to antagonise the public by jailing him and, if they dared to do so, he would starve himself to death.

Kevorkian was eventually charged with the second-degree murder of Thomas Youk who had amyotrophic lateral sclerosis. A video of Youk's suicide on *60 Minutes* enabled the authorities to pursue his conviction. The trial was a farce. Kevorkian insisted on representing himself, appalling even his own supporters with his ineptitude in the court. In 1999 a Michigan court sentenced him to ten to twenty-five years in prison. Suffering from advanced hepatitis C, Kevorkian was released on parole in July 2007, bound not to have any contact with the media.

Kevorkian was always a marginal character in medicine, his pathology career was a failure and his idiosyncratic hobbies and interests did little to provide meaningful engagement with people. Kevorkian's early fascination with the Armenian Genocide facilitated the preoccupation with death and experimentation. There are strong overtones of necromancy in this situation.

Kevorkian's activities received world-wide coverage and it was inevitable that others would take up the cause of assisted suicide. In Australia, Dr Philip Nitschke rose to prominence with the world's first legalisation of assisted euthanasia in the Northern Territory in 1995. Raised in South Australia, Nitschke got a doctorate in laser physics in 1974. He worked as a caretaker of the Kangaroo Island Oceanographic Field Station, an adviser to the Gurindji people, a tram conductor and taxi driver in Melbourne, and as a park ranger in Central Australia. Nitschke studied medicine at Sydney University, graduating in 1989. He worked in Darwin for four years before being dismissed after taking part in protests involving the nuclear powered submarine USS *Houston*. He subsequently established an after-hours medical practice for Northern Territory drug addicts, seeking publicity to pressure the government to provide better facilities.

In 1995 the *Rights of the Terminally Ill Act* legalised euthanasia in Australia's Northern Territory. Nitschke had not been involved in caring for terminally ill people or palliative care in the Territory. Once the Act was passed, he developed the 'Deliverance' machine, a laptop computer which controlled the lethal drug administration to enable the patient to initiate the process. The laptop computer, plastic tubing and a pump-driven syringe filled with barbiturates were held in an old grey suitcase. The computer had an interactive suicide software program. After the patient was hooked up to an intravenous line connected to the computer and the program turned on, a series of three questions appeared on the computer screen:

1. Are you aware that if you go ahead to the last screen and press the 'yes' button, you will be given a lethal dose of medicine and die?
   Yes / No
2. Are you certain you understand that if you proceed and press the 'yes' button on the next screen, you will die?
   Yes / No
3. In 15 seconds you will be given a lethal injection.
   Yes / No

Clicking 'yes' for all three questions activated a syringe driver and a sequential delivery of death-inducing drugs. The method meant that the doctor did not directly administer the fatal dose.

Terminally ill taxi driver Bob Dent sought out Nitschke to become the first patient to die under the new law. To meet the law's requirements, prominent Sydney psychiatrist Dr John Ellard certified that Dent was mentally competent to make a decision to terminate his own life. Dent died on 22 September 1996, the event receiving wide publicity, as did three more cases that Nitschke attended. Describing his response to Dent's death, Nitschke said, 'I felt at the end of it enhanced by the experience. I did not feel in any way that I have done the wrong thing.' Later, indicating a degree of confusion in his own mind, he acknowledged, 'You can't help but feel like an executioner. You get to know people and then you just end up one day killing them.'

The euthanasia law was voided by the Commonwealth government in 1997. Nitschke continued working on different means of administering lethal drugs and seeking ways to get around the legal restrictions. In the tradition of many treatment killers, he soon earned the soubriquet of 'Dr Death'. He established Euthanasia Advisory Clinics and Euthanasia Advisory Workshops in Australian capitals and New Zealand in 2001. The work was funded by donations to EXIT Australia of which he was director. The EXIT Program investigated improved ways of obtaining a death. He developed the CoGenie to end a person's life by delivering carbon monoxide through plastic tubing to the person's nose. He researched substances that had never been approved for patient use which, as they would not be regarded as medications, could be sold in kit form over the internet.

Asked at a 1999 conference about the possibility of teenage access to suicide kits, Nitschke said people should tell the politicians to 'pass the laws we want or we'll sell suicide kits to your kids'. In July 2002, he announced the production of plastic bags with drawstrings that people could put over their heads to commit suicide.

Nitschke's most controversial case was the death of Nancy Crick. A former barmaid, Ms Crick announced that she was planning her suicide because she was dying from bowel cancer. Nitschke organised a rally of 300 people in March 2002 to support her. When Crick arrived at the rally, she was greeted with a standing ovation. Crick became a celebrity. This got the media's attention and TV stations from Japan and the United States wanted to film her death.

Crick picked April 10 for her 'self-deliverance'—the day she would end her life by drug overdose. Then, in late March, she entered the palliative care ward at St Vincents Hospital in Robina. Crick was put on a morphine pump and used analgesic patches. The doctors wanted her to have bowel surgery, but she refused.

Crick killed herself on 22 May 2002. She served the 21 guests who attended champagne, tea and sandwiches. She took an anti-nausea drug to prevent vomiting, followed by a barbiturate overdose, and then swallowed Baileys Cream Liqueur to enhance the effect. She finished with three drags on a cigarette while her guests clapped. It took her twenty minutes to die. Among the 21 onlookers were eight relatives.

Nitschke had flown to Darwin before her death to avoid being legally compromised. Under pressure from the media, Nitschke tried to play down some aspects of the story but it became evident that claims of Crick's advanced illness could not be sustained. The autopsy showed that Crick was free of cancer and Nitschke admitted that both he and Crick knew that she wasn't terminally ill. He argued that her non-terminal condition was 'irrelevant' because she was 'hopelessly ill' with a painful digestive problem. Her family was reported to be shocked by the news.

Nitschke continued to seek outlets and opportunities to market his product. He travelled to New Zealand to address groups and promote his books. He went to America to seek approval for internet publication of his book that had been banned in Australia. It is likely Nitschke's cat-and-mouse game with the authorities will play out for some time to come.

Where a terminal patient is concerned, the issue of euthanasia is beyond objective debate. Intractable pain and suffering negate any argument about ethics. Dehumanisation, if not debility from chemotherapy and radiation, is widely feared by patients and relatives alike. There is no other situation in medicine that lends itself so well to exploitation by a charismatic doctor. Some doctors portray themselves as dedicated and selfless anti-establishment pioneers while adopting increasingly extreme positions. At first their intention is to provide an escape from intolerable suffering for terminal patients; then assistance is extended to patients who have all the ailments of life, often disorders such as depression or anxiety; finally, they offer, on libertarian or humanitarian grounds, the opportunity to anyone who so desires to end their life. Constantly provoking the authorities permits them to portray themselves as victims of a bureaucratic or uncaring state appar-atus. Attracting an admiring and defensive cohort of followers, they achieve heroic or martyr status when prevented from continuing their work or apprehended by the state.

It can be said with certainty that were doctors engaged in such practices permitted to continue unabated, there would be treatment killing at an unprecedented level in our times.

13

Psychiatrist of the Bosnian Genocide

Dr Radovan Karadzic

Do not think that you will not perhaps lead the Muslim people into annihilation because the Muslim people cannot defend themselves if there is war. How will you prevent everyone from being killed in Bosnia-Herzegovina?

Dr Radovan Karadzic, 4 March 1992

One of the most notorious medical involvements in genocide occurred in the final decade of the twentieth century. The 1992–1995 war in the Republic of Bosnia-Herzegovina heralded the return of the spectre of mass murder to Europe.

Concentration camps, not seen since the Nazis, were re-established. An appalling and destructive war followed, in which Bosnian Serb forces committed numerous atrocities in their pursuit to ethnically cleanse the territory.

Psychiatrist Dr Radovan Karadzic became the president of Bosnian Serbia in 1992, and he proceeded to ruthlessly mastermind the Bosnian Genocide. The full extent of killing carried out by Bosnian Serb forces will never be known, but it is estimated that 250,000 people died and a million more were uprooted from their homes, forced to become refugees. The damage and destruction wrought during the war will take decades to repair. The casualties, survivors and victims of shooting, torture, rape and forced relocation—many of whom are now dispersed around the world as refugees—will suffer for the rest of their lives.

While fighting in the former Yugoslavia occurred on other fronts—with appalling consequences for the civilian population—the Bosnian War was unique in one aspect: the role of psychiatrists in establishing the Bosnian Serb Party and leading the revanchist campaign against the civilian population of Bosnia-Herzegovina. The term *ethnic cleansing* was coined to explain the use of military and paramilitary force against civilians to move them out of territories claimed by the Serbs. Furthermore, psychiatric knowledge was used to plan the terror tactics behind ethnic cleansing. In the course of the conflict, Bosnian Serb forces committed various acts of violence, chiefly against Muslims.

Following the break-up of Yugoslavia, nationalist leaders in Croatia (Tujman) and Serbia (Milosevic) were determined to expand their territories by a variety of means, including ethnic cleansing. The multi-ethnic state of Bosnia-Herzegovina was the prime goal as the two states manoeuvred to redress ancient scores and drive away other nationals. Slobodan Milosevic encouraged the development of irredentist groups in Bosnia as proxies for his goal to create Greater Serbia. The chief proxy was the Serbian Democratic Party of Bosnia-Herzegovina, known as the SDS. The SDS was established in 1990 by Dr Jovan Raskovic, head of psychiatry at the Sarajevo mental hospital in Croatia. The SDS had many health professionals as members.

Raskovic was born in Knin in 1929. He studied medicine at the University of Zagreb, obtaining his psychiatric speciality in 1962 and working at Sibenik Hospital. Raskovic published widely in international psychiatric journals. His early papers on conventional psychiatric topics give little indication of his political views. Later titles like 'Narcissism and Depersonalisation' became increasingly subjective, the most notorious being 'Luda Zemlja' (The Mad Country). Raskovic used psychiatric language to explain and justify Serbian aggression, while simultaneously dehumanising the opposition, especially Muslims. 'As a result of Muslim laws regarding the hygiene of the anal channel', he wrote, 'Muslims were disposed to gather property and behave aggressively'. Croats, he added, were psychologically driven to challenge the power of Serbs, the 'nation of tragic destiny'. The connection between heaven and national destiny created 'conditions for the religious destiny of an ethnical being'.

Raskovic became a public figure, using demagoguery to stir up the crowds. He fell out with Tujman, the Croatian leader, when he refused to join the government and had to stand down. He was replaced by Sarajevo psychiatrist Dr Radovan Karadzic, who surprised many by becoming head of the SDS.

Radovan Karadzic was born in 1945, the eldest of three children, in the mountain village of Petnjica, district of Savnik, Montenegro. His parents were of peasant stock. His father,

Vuk Karadzic, described as an itinerant with a history of incest and theft, was sentenced to death by the Partisans for his activities as a Chetnik during World War II; Chetniks were the nationalist guerrillas who fought against both Nazi occupiers and the communist Yugoslav Partisans. Vuk Karadzic was pardoned after serving time in Tito's prisons. Many of the Karadzic extended family were killed by the fascist Ustasha Partisans, a legacy that must have been hard to ignore.

At fifteen, Karadzic moved to the city of Sarajevo, living in a multi-ethnic neighbourhood and mixing comfortably with Serbian, Croat and Muslim neighbours. Neighbours recalled a shy farm boy wearing a grimy white pullover knitted with wool from his village. He seems to have been popular, if not endearing; they gave him free haircuts, baklava and shoe repairs. His striking looks—he was over 1.8 metres tall with a Byronic shock of hair—attracted attention, and he became a serial seducer of women. In 1965, Karadzic, with a high school diploma from the medical vocational school, studied first nursing, then medicine, at the University of Sarajevo, receiving his degree in 1971 and going on to qualify in psychiatry. He joined and left the Communist Party, and married Ljiljana Zelen, a psychiatrist from an upper-class Sarajevo family. The couple had two children. With suspicious amounts of money at his disposal, he was thought to be a police informer and shunned by many.

From his student days, Karadzic wrote children's stories and Serbian folk songs, giving performances on the gusle (a single-string Serbian instrument) in public and on radio. Karadzic published several volumes of poetry and received state prizes. His work included apocalyptic and rebarbative images of violence, such as the charmingly titled *Let's Go Down to the Town and Kill Some Scum* (1971). The self-fulfilling poem

Sarajevo described the city burning in a 'blood-soaked tide'. The local literati, however, did not share Karadzic's opinion of his talent. According to writer Marko Vesovic: 'We had considered his case hopeless as far as literature is concerned.' Never one to be deterred by adverse reviews, Karadzic's fourth volume (1990) 'revealed an obsession with blood and violence', the shining example being *The Morning Hand-Grenade*.

In 1974 Karadzic attended Columbia University for a year. According to an interview, he took courses in psychotherapy and American poetry—although there is no record of his enrolment in any courses. This again raised questions about the funding and motives for his trip. It was rumoured that KOS (the counter-intelligence agency of the former Yugoslavia) had sponsored him.

Another example of Karadzic's boundless confidence in his own ability, despite his complete lack of sporting experience, was his appointment as team psychiatrist for the Sarajevo and the Belgrade Red Star soccer teams. Despite bombarding the players with mass hypnosis, they failed to win.

With a preference for scotch whisky and gambling heavily in casinos, Karadzic was always seeking extra income, selling medical certificates to those who wanted state pensions. In 1985 he was sentenced to three years in prison for using a $100 000 grant to build his chicken farm in nearby Pale, the ski resort town 16 kilometres from Sarajevo. Karadzic claimed he was a political prisoner and used his contacts to ensure that he only spent eleven months in prison before returning to work at the hospital.

In 1987 he presented a paper analysing a poem about bizarre bodily mutilation to a psychotherapy conference. In 1989 Karadzic became head of the Serbian Green Party, a grim irony in view of his later despoiling large tracts of Bosnia.

In 1990 he unexpectedly emerged from political obscurity as head of the Serbian Democratic Party of Bosnia-Herzegovina, or SDS. His aggressive nationalism and vicious anti-Muslim rhetoric surprised many who until then had regarded him as unscrupulous but apolitical.

> You want to take Bosnia and Herzegovina down the same highway to hell and suffering that Slovenia and Croatia are travelling. Do not think that you will not lead Bosnia and Herzegovina into hell, and do not think that you will not perhaps lead the Muslim people into annihilation, because the Muslims cannot defend themselves if there is war—How will you prevent everyone from being killed in Bosnia and Herzegovina?
>
> Dr Radovan Karadzic,
> in a speech to the Bosnian Parliament

The last record of Karadzic working in psychiatry is in March 1992 at the Nedjo Zec psychiatric clinic in Kosevo Hospital, Sarajevo. In the last year, he was always accompanied by bodyguards, who distressed staff and patients by insisting on body searches. Karadzic's availability became increasingly limited, unhappy patients were always waiting outside his office and his supervisor, Dr Ceric, requested he take leave. He planned to write a book on depression but, like so many of his claims, this never eventuated.

In 1990 the SDS proclaimed a network of 'Serb Autonomous Regions' which from 1992 orchestrated the removal of all Muslims and Croats in the Serbs' path. As Yugoslavia moved towards dissolution, Karadzic warned that if Bosnia and Herzegovina declared independence, Bosnian Serbs would secede and seek union with Serbia. In April 1992 civil war erupted. Karadzic became president of the Bosnian Serb Republic (Republika Srpska) based in the self-proclaimed capital of Pale. By December 1992, Serbs had seized about 70 per cent of Bosnia and Herzegovina.

Why not? It's all strange here, nothing is normal.
Psychiatrist Dr Ferhid Mujanovic,
after Kosovo Hospital was shelled by the Serbians

Karadzic's direct involvement in the atrocities is undeniable. In constant contact with Milosevic, he coordinated strategy with General Ratko Mladic, his military leader. A remarkably public frontman of the regime, he would conduct interviews near the firing artillery dressed in military fatigues, his shock of hair looming above his defiant pout. He blatantly lied at press conferences while his soldiers laid siege to Sarajevo, going from village to village locking families inside houses and setting them on fire, and forcing women into detention camps where they were gang-raped. Karadzic's training in group therapy influenced his choice of terror tactics. He authorised the siege of Sarajevo, shelling the homes of his colleagues and killing patients in their beds at the hospital where he worked. There are also allegations that he witnessed and participated in torture at Bosnian Serb concentration camps.

In 1993, Serbian psychiatrists published *The Stresses of War*, documenting the effects of the war on the Serbian people. While condemning war crimes and genocide, the authors' bias was evident in their discussion of the rape of non-Serb women. Firstly, the number of victims was played down; secondly, the tendentious allegation was posited that the rapes could not have been ordered by officers—because no one can get an erection on command. The authors alleged that the international media 'satanised' the Serbian people, preparing the way for genocide against them. In an ironic reversal of Dr Raskovic's writings, they alleged that psychiatry was misused to 'spread hatred against the Serbian people'. *Sanctions*, published in 1994, portrayed international sanctions as a prelude to Serbian genocide. By ignoring the aggressive role of the Serbian government in the Bosnian War, the psychiatrists acted as genocide apologists.

Following highly publicised atrocities, the West reluctantly intervened. Milosevic signed the Dayton Peace Accords in December 1995, effectively shutting the door on the Bosnian Serb leadership. The Accords partitioned Bosnia and Herzegovina into Serb and Muslim-Croat areas and ended the war. The political tide turned, and an international warrant for his arrest was issued against Karadzic who resigned in July 1996. Surrounded by heavily armed bodyguards, Karadzic ensconced himself in a remote mountain fastness in Eastern Bosnia, swearing he would never stand trial. Like so many of his promises, this only lasted until the fall of Milosevic, when he went underground in Serbia.

The longer Karadzic remained free, the more his heroic status among the Serbs escalated. Calendars showing his image hung at bus stations. Despite being on the run, he could not resist the temptation to publish another book of poetry and affectionate letters to his wife, a roman à clef that must have amazed those who knew his usual devotion to marital fidelity. One Christmas, thousands of Bosnian Serbs received a text-message holiday greeting from Karadzic on their mobile phones.

Karadzic's arrest in July 2008 after nine years on the run was no accident. A new Serbian government committed to joining the European Union sent over a few policemen to hook him off a suburban bus. Working openly as an alternative practitioner-guru under the teasingly alliterative title of 'Dr Dragan David Dabic', Karadzic promoted a weird theory of bioenergetics. His familiar jut-jawed face obscured by a dense beard, hair bound in a ponytail, looking like nothing more than an aging hippy running a market stall selling dope paraphernalia, he ran group meetings and spoke on a local radio station. Showing that old habits die hard, he had a close association with an attractive divorcee who coyly denied any involvement and promptly became a media celebrity.

At the police station Karadzic requested to be shorn and from the hairy chrysalis emerged the familiar blustering figure who harangued reporters about protecting fellow Serbs from Turks (Muslims) while shelling the hapless burghers of his home town of Sarajevo. Blog sites described it as Karadzic's bad-hair day. Promptly shunted off to a cell at The Hague to face charges of crimes against humanity, Karadzic commenced with the predictable set-piece that he did not recognise the jurisdiction of the court, was a victim of an international conspiracy and, in any event, had been promised an exemption from prosecution by the Americans.

Karadzic's trajectory from ordinary hospital psychiatrist to genocidal murder shows an uncanny resonance with that of Hitler. Both came from a rural background to spend their early youth in multi-ethnic cosmopolitan surroundings—Hitler in Vienna, Karadzic in Sarajevo—over-compensating for their marginal origins by adopting a super-nationalistic posture. In Vienna Hitler mixed with people of all backgrounds including Jews, his murderous racism only coming to the fore in 1919. In Sarajevo, Karadzic socialised with Muslims, Bosnians, Montenegrins, Croats and Jews. His Muslim friend and colleague Dr Ceric mentioned how Karadzic had sent birthday greetings to his mother in 1990, while already promoting the ethnic cleansing of Bosnian Serbia.

Hitler, who failed to get into art or architecture school, regarded himself as an artist. While able to qualify as a psychiatrist, Karadzic had a similar grandiose and romantic vision of himself. His ambivalence about finding a suitable role to express his abilities was significant; interspersed with ecology, chicken farming (an occupation he shared with Heinrich Himmler), fraudulent money-making schemes, soccer coaching and a stint in jail, he continued to work as a psychiatrist (and intended to write a book on depression) until 1992, when the war broke out and his genocidal career reached its apogee.

We do not know why Karadzic chose medicine and psychiatry but, noting his elevated view of himself, it is likely he saw this as a way to demonstrate his superiority to the world. His psychiatric work was 'ordinary'. Patients complained that he was not interested in their problems while colleagues said that he provoked psychotic patients. When a psychopathic patient with a knife ran loose in the ward, breaking the windows, Karadzic retreated to his room, leaving a nurse to disarm and calm the patient. His colleagues said that he was always late, diagnosed everybody with masked depression and never completed case reports. His colleagues were aware of his grandiose, if unrealistic, plans; the frequent assertions that he would become a famous psychiatrist or poet were regarded with scepticism. The ease with which he took to selling fake medical certificates and prescriptions indicates a contempt for professional standards and lack of scruples in attaining his goals.

It is inevitable that questions will be raised about Karadzic's mental state. It was claimed he had a nervous breakdown after his wife became pregnant. Despite his confident exterior, there was an underlying anxiety and he continually chewed his nails. Marko Vesovic described him as a psychopath, 'a man without a core'. Dr Ceric said that in the springtime and autumn Karadzic was depressed and 'a little bit, sometimes euphoric' during summer and winter. His drinking, womanising, gambling and indiscriminate spending are indicative of a flamboyant and reckless nature with strong elements of opportunism. Warren Zimmerman, the last US ambassador to Yugoslavia, regarded him as barking mad, obsessed with violence and in need of psychiatric treatment.

What cannot be denied is Karadzic's capacity for gross denial. Dr Ceric described Karadzic's most distinctive quality as the 'mechanism for the falsification of reality'. Karadzic could explain any event related to the conflict between Serbs and Muslims in terms of his own world view. 'He doesn't live in reality,' said Dr Ceric. 'At the time there was a joke among our colleagues and our nurses that one day in the future, it's possible that Radovan would come to the clinic early in the morning and say, "Okay I'm back and I'm not guilty of nothing—or everything, everyone else is guilty... the Americans or something... so how about some tea or coffee".'

After the ceasefire, Karadzic continued to maintain that he was free of guilt for war atrocities, blaming it on Muslim forces or the international media. In the face of overwhelming evidence of murderous atrocities by Bosnian Serb forces, he constantly reiterated that there was not one shred of evidence to support these claims and that (again) the atrocities had been carried out by Muslims against their own people. He alleged Muslims destroyed the famous National Library with its irreplaceable cultural treasures because it was a Christian building. Far from Sarajevo being under siege by Serbian forces for two years, he declared, Muslim guns were there to prevent citizens from breaking out of the city. The most disturbing example is his response to the killing of 68 civilians by a mortar shell at the Markale marketplace on 5 February 1994. Karadzic insisted the corpses had been taken from the Sarajevo morgues and blown up by Muslim forces 'to gain the sympathy of the world'. As proof, he made the ludicrous claim that the corpses had ice in their ears.

From his rather ordinary career as a psychiatrist until 1992 to his period as genocidal leader, Radovan Karadzic displayed an extraordinary degree of rampant megalomania associated with reckless opportunism in which the instincts of an extreme gambler were unchallenged by any restraint or fear of the consequences. The paradox is that Karadzic lived in multi-ethnic Sarajevo in Bosnia, a situation that only existed because of the rule of communists under Tito—the same communists who had killed his relatives during the war and imprisoned his father. In psychological terms, it can be explained as identification with the aggressor.

At The Hague, Karadzic faces a trial carefully adjusted to ensure quick conviction and deny him opportunities for grandstanding, followed by jailing, almost certainly for the rest of his life. This will enhance his cult status and provide him with yet another stage on which to demonstrate his heroism to the homeland cheer squad. The circumstances will be eminently suitable for him to portray himself as a nationalist martyr, more volumes of execrable poetry will surely follow, worship of his brave wife will escalate to the level of Mariolatry and, with the passing of time, he will surely segue into his final character: the Balkan Nelson Mandela.

These are truly scenes from hell, written on the darkest pages of human history.

Judge Fouad Riad,
reviewing the Srebrenica killings

Karadzic now stands indicted as a suspected war criminal for crimes against humanity and genocide, the first doctor so indicted since the Nuremberg Doctors' Trial in 1946. These crimes include the indiscriminate murder of civilians, killing 68 civilians in the Markale marketplace, the use of 248 United Nations peacekeepers as human shields, and the murder of up to 7500 people under UN protection at Srebrenica.

In 1993, the American Psychiatric Association passed a motion condemning Karadzic for 'brutal and inhumane actions'. The condemnation was issued with 'particular offence, urgency and horror because, by membership and training, Dr Karadzic claims membership in our profession'.

Dr Radovan Karadzic's short reign as president of the Bosnian Serb Republic leaves an appalling legacy. The full extent of the destruction wrought by his forces during the war will never be fully known. While many aspects of Karadzic's personality remain deeply enigmatic, his uncontrolled opportunism, grandiose self-image, wild and profligate nature, and grotesque capacity for self-deception were clearly displayed. There was nothing banal about Karadzic's course—it was megalomania of an extraordinary degree.

14

Genocidal doctors

Anyone who sees and paints a sky green and fields blue
ought to be sterilised.

Adolf Hitler

Doctors as a group are highly susceptible to carrying out
appalling acts on behalf of the state. Political medical murderers
reverse the process of patients seeking help from a doctor,
instead misusing their medical skills in the most horrendous
fashion to abuse a vulnerable minority on the basis of
nationalism. Like the rest of the population, doctors have a
range of political views; as an especially conservative group,
they would be more likely to support nationalistic movements.
Religious belief is no guide, as Protestant and Jewish (Africa),
Roman Catholic (South America, Bosnia), Orthodox Serb

(Bosnia) and Muslim (Turkey, Yugoslavia) doctors have been indicted in state abuses.

In the course of their training, they are desensitised by dissecting corpses, attending post-mortems and dealing with death as a routine, daily event. In the process, they learn to develop a 'medical self' with a professional demeanour that shows no sign of their underlying feelings. Added to this is a feature seldom noted. Of all the professions, doctors have the most protracted gestation. They develop great expertise in a very narrow field while experiencing little of the real world. Much of this is done in a hierarchical environment where their elite status as doctors is continually acknowledged. This results in doctors who are over-burdened with medical knowledge, inexperienced in dealing with real-life dilemmas, and who have an inculcated belief that they represent an elite profession and a deep-seated respect for authority and hierarchy. As a group, they accept, without questioning, the status quo.

The growing involvement of doctors in state-sponsored crimes stems from the concept of *total war*. From discreet conflicts of the nineteenth century involving only designated combatants, by Hitler's time the distinction between civilian and military was blurred beyond recognition, and atrocities against the civilian population were regarded as an essential means of waging war. Murder of the civilian population was a notable feature of the struggle during World War II; in Yugoslavia for example, more civilians were killed by the opposing Chetnik and Ustasha resistance forces than by the Nazi invaders.

Mass psychology has been utilised with lethal effectiveness, from the propaganda mobilisation of the population to the use of terror tactics in combat. It is inevitable that psychiatrists and psychologists would assume leading roles in propagandising, planning and waging aggressive war, rather then restricting themselves to their professional roles.

The participation of doctors in state terror started in the French Revolution with Dr Jean-Paul Marat. The Swiss-born Marat, like other marginal figures in history, was more fanatic than the local revolutionaries. His comrade Robert commented that 'His malady consists in believing he is the only patriot of France, and it is a delirium'. Marat trained in medicine in Bordeaux, Paris, Holland and England. His medical work was well regarded, especially papers on dermatology and ophthalmology. Marat returned to Paris in 1777 with a reputation as a doctor, scientist and political thinker. He was soon known as 'Doctor of the Incurables' and his optical and electrical experiments interested Benjamin Franklin.

However, Marat failed to gain membership in the prestigious Academy of Sciences, a slight he felt deeply, and which fed his sense of persecution. A distinctive figure, Marat was extremely short, raising the inevitable comparisons with Napoleon. His dress and appearance were untidy, showing his disregard for social convention, perhaps a way to identify with the *sansculottes* proletariat. When the revolution arrived, it became an instrument for revenge. In July 1790 Marat wrote 'Five or six hundred heads cut off would have assured your repose, freedom and happiness. A false humanity has held your arms and suspended your blows; because of this millions of your brothers will lose their lives.'

In combating enemies of the state, Marat was remorseless, displaying the paranoid logic that became a feature of twentieth-century dictatorships, seeing the number of enemies constantly multiplying: 'In order to assure public tranquillity, 200,000 heads must be cut off.' In this regard, he anticipated another (much-lauded) revolutionary doctor, Ernesto 'Che' Guevara, who attended firing squads to dispatch his many victims. Marat approved of massacres of 'enemies of the Revolution' and established the 'Committee of Surveillance' to 'root out anti-revolutionaries', composing the death lists from which innocent and the guilty alike were executed. He ceaselessly issued pamphlets warning the citizenry of plots to assassinate them in their beds, leading to massacres of inmates, prisoners and mental asylum patients, in addition to the aristocracy. In the end, even Marat's allies became uncomfortable. 'The revolution is consuming its own children,' said one.

Marat suffered from severe itching, requiring him to spend long periods in the bath; a special shoe-shaped tub was designed to accommodate him. This led to speculation that his skin ailment was due to syphilis, eczema or psoriasis, but the most likely cause was seborrheic dermatitis. Marat received visitors while he was in the bath and, in a form of rough justice was, as it were, killed by his disease as he was soaking when he was stabbed to death in 1793.

After Marat, it may have appeared that doctors had restricted their political activities, but evidence is now starting to emerge that this was not the case. New research has begun to expose the role of doctors in administering prisoner of war camps in the American Civil War and concentration camps during the Anglo-Boer War. By the end of the nineteenth century, a new and ultimately rebarbative concept was taking hold, particularly amongst German, Swedish, British and American doctors. This was eugenics, the idea that some individuals were biologically inferior and could destroy the integrity of the human race through inferior blood. This concept reached its horrifying consummation in the Nazi euthanasia of mental patients and the Holocaust.

German culture was preoccupied with racial notions of blood and stock, so it was natural that eugenics would filter through to the medical fraternity. A leading proponent was medical anthropologist Dr Eugene Fischer, the driving force behind a forgotten episode in history, the genocide of the Herero people in German South West Africa. The horror of this war, intended to eliminate the Herero people after the Herero uprising against the Germans in 1904, is still difficult to contemplate. However, after the Germans were ousted from the area in World War I, it slipped off the historical radar. Fischer, however, continued to be an influential force in German medicine in the period leading up to World War II. The consequences were dire.

The systematic participation of doctors in state terror commenced in 1915 with the Armenian Genocide in Turkey. Many doctors had leading roles in the Ittihadist Party that came to power in 1908. The leading figures were Dr Behaeddin Sakir and Dr Mehmett Nazim, who played a pivotal role in the establishment and deployment of the Special Organization units, extermination squads staffed by violent criminals. Sakir worked at one time as the chief physician of Soloniki Municipal Hospital and Nazim, described as 'a doctor by profession and not without promise', in what must be regarded as one of the most misguided appointments in the history of medicine, was the professor of Legal (Ethical) Medicine at Istanbul Medical School. Utterly unrepentant to the end of his life, Nazim was thought to have committed a million murders.

With the onset of World War I, a number of doctors, as governors of the Eastern Provinces, led Special Organization units against the Armenians. Hundreds of thousands of men, women and children were rounded up and killed by a range of brutal means, including drowning in the sea, throat slitting, poisoning, injections of gasoline and phenol and being buried alive. Other forms of coercion, such as mass rape, looting and destruction of homes were employed, a fore-runner of the ethnic cleansing in Bosnia. After the war, there was testimony that victims were led off in groups and slaughtered by butchers like cattle in an abattoir.

Medical personnel did not merely supervise proceedings but were directly involved in the killings, often participating in torture. Dr Mehmed Reşid, the 'Executioner Governor', was involved in the 'deportation' of 120,000 Armenians from his province, in addition to embezzling thousands of pounds. Reşid's brutality was extraordinary, including smashing skulls, nailing red-hot horseshoes onto the victim's chest, and crucifying victims on makeshift crosses. Sadistic cruelty was demonstrated by ophthalmologists who gave eye drops to children to make them blind. Other doctors, describing their victims as subhuman, used them as guinea pigs to infect with a range of diseases. Hundreds of victims were injected with blood from typhus cases.

Military pharmacist Mehmed Hasan (Ezaci) was accused of murdering 2000 Armenian labour battalion soldiers and allowing his men to rape 250 women and children. Dr Ali Said killed thousands of infants, adults and pregnant women by administering poison as liquid medicine, and ordering drowning at sea of patients who refused the 'medicine'. Dr Tevfik Rusdü (Aras) was directed to dispose of corpses of the victims. Mass graves were seeded with quicklime to destroy the bodies. A woman later gave evidence that his infant victims were taken to a purported steam bath and killed with a toxic gas, an ominous precursor of the gas chambers of Auschwitz and Treblinka.

Following their defeat, the Turkish government was directed by the Allies to try the perpetrators and the main offenders were sentenced to death. Many escaped this fate by going into exile; several were assassinated by Armenian agents in Paris; a few committed suicide. In the end, only three participants were executed. When Dr Mehmat Kemal was hanged in April 1919, medical students from Istanbul University demonstrated in protest. The Kemalist government then turned its back on the issue and the collective Turkish denial that the genocide had ever occurred took hold. Kemal is today commemorated by a statue in a public square.

In the years afterwards, looking at the issue from radically different moral standpoints, Hitler and Churchill noted that everyone forgot the matter before long and Armenia was destined to slip into historical amnesia.

The Armenian Genocide set the ground for the most notorious examples of medical complicity in state abuses: the Nazi doctors who participated in euthanasia and genocide, and the Japanese doctors who practised biological warfare. Included among the former were psychiatrists, who in carrying out Hitler's euthanasia program on their patients, appear to have been in a state of complete moral disarray. The German medical profession did not need any pushing to accept Nazi ideology after Hitler came into power in 1933; in fact, they positively jumped into the hands of the government. Doctors had the largest representation in the Nazi Party of all occupational groups.

No other profession submitted so quickly, or in such great numbers to the Nazis. The German medical profession acquiesced in the drive to expel all Jewish doctors from the profession without a murmur. Nazi racial theories were accepted without question. The Nazi physician was designated a 'selector' to improve the health of the nation by removing 'inferiors'. Eugenics and racial hygiene were compulsory subjects in medical schools.

The first steps towards genocide began in 1938 with euthanasia: the selection of patients with incurable physical or mental disease. From here the process accelerated with the move to exterminate psychiatric patients on eugenic grounds. The program to kill 'unworthy' adults, known as Aktion or Operation T4, after the Berlin address of Nazi headquarters at Tiergarten 4, was directed by a large medical and ancillary bureaucracy based at six centres in Germany and Austria. There was a complex system of reassuring letters and falsified death certificates to relatives. Jews alone required no medical paperwork or phoney diagnoses to be murdered.

Before long, doctors were experimenting with means of killing such as phenol injections, then carbon monoxide gassing. Gas chambers were introduced to dispose of 'incurables' from the mental hospitals of the Reich. Word of what was happening soon reached the population. Public demonstrations took place and Count von Galen, the Catholic bishop of Münster, delivered the famous sermon in which he declared the program was a blasphemy against God:

> Poor unproductive people if you wish, but does this mean that they have lost their right to live?

Psychiatrists Karl Bonhoeffer and Gottfried Ewald resisted, as did several Protestant pastors involved in mental hospitals. Paul-Gerhard Braune, the only objector who was arrested, wrote to Hitler condemning the very concept of *life unworthy of life* and warning that unless the 'intolerable' program was halted, the moral foundations of the nation would be undermined.[1] In the only example of the Nazi leadership bowing to public protest, it was announced the program was indefinitely suspended in 1941. In fact, it continued, but in a more discreet fashion. By 1945, Operation T4, directed and run by medical personnel, was responsible for the deaths of

200,000 psychiatric patients, concentration camp patients, patients with severe depression and 'nonconformists'.

With the onset of the war, the German medical profession sank to hitherto unimaginable depths of depravity. Large-scale experimental programs were conducted at leading medical research institutes using *untermenschen*, or alleged subhuman subjects. No coercion was required to get doctors to work in experimental institutes or concentration camps; there was no shortage of well-paid volunteers. These doctors lost the last vestiges of moral sensibility when they served in fighting SS units. The doctors did 'selections' at the death camps, dividing victims into those destined for immediate extermination in the gas ovens, and those who could do some useful work for a while or be used in experiments. The operation of the crematoria, determination of when the victims were dead and individual means of killing were all done under medical supervision.

Jews, Gypsies, Slavs, homosexuals and the disabled were regarded as subhuman, targets for annihilation or exploitation, most notoriously in medical experiments. The experiments were beyond belief. The subjects were treated like insensate animals with brutal surgery, freezing to death and injections with lethal bacteria or various poisons.

The official approach was that doctors, not other camp officials, should supervise the selection process. Their responsibilities were arduous. They included not only selection on the ramp and supervision of the killings, but selections within the camp, direct killing by injections (mostly by phenol), certifying death at individual executions, signing false death certificates, overseeing tooth extraction from corpses, controlling epidemics, performing abortions, observing floggings, offering advice on cremation and other means of corpse disposal, and advice on controlling the influx of prisoners into the camp itself, which of course affected the proportion of arrivals sent straight to their deaths.

Selection duty on the ramp was accompanied at Auschwitz by a literal numbing: the doctors drank heavily in what became a carefully observed group ritual, and encouraged shaken or reluctant newcomers to get drunk with them. The doctors jestingly referred to *Therapia Magna Auschwitzensis* (shortened to TM), their unofficial euphemism for the gas chamber. At the lowest level, 'numbing' was only an extension of self-protective attitudes always present in the medical profession: the hardening to horror required in any casualty ward, or the 'sawbones' humour common among surgeons. At the 'euthanasia' centre of Hadamar, a drunken party with music and mock sermons was held in the cremation room to 'celebrate' the ten thousandth victim.

No one more epitomised the medical horror of the concentration camps than Dr Joseph Mengele. He started off as a medical researcher interested in congenital defects. He was wounded in action serving with an SS mountain warfare unit. Unfit for front-line service as a result of his injuries, Mengele went to Auschwitz, where he became notorious as the 'Angel of Death', that soubriquet so often used to describe medical killers. He would stand at the railway station wearing a white coat and gloves, indicating with his cane who would live and who would die. Mengele's experiments were sadistic and inhumane. He was obsessed with twins, on whom he experimented without restraint. At times, he could be solicitous and caring to his victims; on other occasions, he was brutal and sadistic, shooting people who displeased him on the spot.

Mengele left an indelible impression; always impeccably dressed, smiling pleasantly or whistling Puccini as he distributed death, sometimes dashing into the oncoming torrent of human beings shouting: 'Get those twins over here!' In the medical blocks, Mengele's unpredictability terrified the inmates. His kindness towards some of 'his children', gypsies or twins or children with eyes of contrasting pigment, at times even seemed genuine.

Mengele, who after the war escaped with the assistance of the Vatican to South America, died in obscurity, having evaded all attempts to bring him to justice. According to his son he never repented or regretted what he had done.

After the war, a misleading impression arose that concentration camp doctors were marginal characters, either misfits or psychopaths in the profession. This was far from the truth. Some of the most prominent specialists in Germany were compromised by their work in the research institutes. Leading medical academics involved in wide-ranging abuses included Dr Julius Hallervorden, director of the prestigious Kaiser-Wilhelm Institute, who collected the brains of euthanasia victims for his neuropathological collection. Dr Eduard Pernkopf of Vienna led the purge of Jewish doctors from the medical faculty and acquired anatomy specimens from victims of Nazi terror. These were used in his renowned textbook of anatomy, which has remained in print. Psychiatrist Carl Schneider of Heidelberg studied victims before they were murdered and then dissected their brains. Gynaecologist Dr Hermann Stieve used women prisoners to study the effect of stress on the menstrual cycle— the stress being their impending execution—and studied their pelvic organs after death. Dr Hermann Voss of Pozen used the bodies of executed Gestapo victims for his dissection classes and sold the skeletons for profit.

The Nuremberg medical trials were held from 25 October 1946 to 20 August 1947, a belated attempt to deal with unprecedented medical abuses. Among the 'crimes committed in the guise of scientific research' were high-altitude experiments, sea water experiments, infectious diseases including epidemic jaundice, typhus and gas gangrene, sterilisation experiments, poison experiments and collection of Jewish skeletons.

Of the 23 doctors and scientists who faced trial at Nuremberg, only two were recognised academics. Statements from the doctors indicated how they lost their moral bearings as they were swept up in the grotesque Nazi political culture. Seduced by the power of utilitarian thought and arguments, they allied their professional skills with the annihilating process of a despotic government. Fifteen defendants were found guilty, seven executed and eight sentenced to prison. The Nuremberg Declaration established criteria to ensure that the abuse of human beings for experimentation would never happen again.

Regardless of world-wide revulsion at what had occurred, there was no systematic attempt to deal with the problem, and numerous figures in the German medical establishment escaped without censure and continued their work. Despite the official policy of de-Nazification, German medicine carried on as if nothing had ever happened. The president of the World Medical Association for 1973–74 was Dr Ernst Fromm, a former member of both the SA and SS. In 1992, the president-elect was Dr Hans-Joachim Sewering, a Nazi Party member who had served in the SS and was linked to the death of a fourteen-year-old girl; he was forced to step down when his history was publicised. It then took a public campaign to reveal that German medical schools were still using anatomical collections that came from murdered prisoners.

In the words of one analyst, the Nuremberg experience shows 'the profession carries within it the seeds of its own destruction'.

If it seems impossible to imagine abuses equal to those of the German doctors, Japanese medical abuses were just as bad. After the invasion of Manchuria in 1931, the appalling Unit 731 of the Japanese Imperial Army carried out hideous and unspeakably cruel experiments on thousands of people. Other units operating in a similar fashion include Unit 543 (Hailar), Unit 773 (Songo unit), Unit 100 (Changchun), Unit 1644 (Nanjing), Unit 1855 (Beijing), Unit 8604 (Guangzhou) and Unit 9420 (Singapore). There is constant speculation (covered up after the war) that a camp at Mukden, Manchuria, housing American, British, Australian and New Zealand POWs was used for experiments.

Unit 731 was created by Lieutenant-General Ishii Shiro, who must surely qualify as the worst psychopath in the history of medicine. A fanatic nationalist trained in microbiology, Shiro was obsessed with biological and chemical warfare. Heavy drinking binges, compulsive womanising and patronage of Tokyo's leading geisha houses give some idea of his sense of restraint, indicating a lack of self-control and possibly manic streak in his nature.

In 1928 Shiro undertook a two-year tour of the West to study the effects of biological warfare and chemical warfare. Early in his military career, he invented a water filter to be used by soldiers in the field. At a demonstration to Emperor Hirohito, he urinated in it, gormlessly offering the filtrate to the emperor to drink. When (unsurprisingly) it was refused, he drank it himself.

Indicating Shiro's enduring interest in matters hydrolocical, in 1936 a huge compound—rivalling the Auschwitz-Birkenau death camp in size—was built in Pingfan, near Harbin in northern China. The official name for Unit 731 was the Water Filtration Bureau. It housed administrative buildings, laboratories, workers' dormitories, barracks, a special prison to house human test subjects and a mortuary building. Three giant furnaces cremated the human carcasses.

A special project, code-named Maruta, gathered test subjects from the surrounding population. Among abuses performed at Unit 731 was the freezing of limbs of chained prisoners, infecting hundreds of villages with anthrax, plague and cholera, and performing live vivisection. It is estimated there were 3000 deaths of Chinese prisoners, in addition to 250,000 deaths from biological warfare experiments. The hapless victims were referred to as 'logs' by the doctors on the grounds that killing a prisoner was the same as cutting down a tree.

A member of the unit described how patients infected with plague were cut up while alive. Some victims were slowly burned alive with repeated jolts of 20,000 volts of electricity. When Shiro wanted a human brain to experiment upon, guards would hold down a prisoner and cleave open his skull with an axe. The organ would be torn out and rushed to Shiro's laboratory.

Shiro's ambition to use biological weapons in the Pacific conflict did not come to pass as the Japanese forces were driven back by the Allies. When it was clear that surrender was imminent, he ordered his men to blow up the compound to destroy evidence of their experimentation. As a final indication of their barberous contempt, they also released the plague-infected animals into the countryside.

After the war, the American occupiers in Japan colluded in a cover-up of the medical abuses. Shiro and other key personnel were granted immunity in return for sharing their research with American scientists. Dr Masaji Kitano, who succeeded Shiro as commander of the unit, became head of the Green Cross, Japan's largest pharmaceutical company. A number of doctors held senior university posts. Shiro died, free of prosecution or public taint, in 1959. To this day, the Japanese government has refused to acknowledge or apologise for the medical abuses.

The Hippocratic Oath declares: 'I will use treatment to help the sick according to my ability and judgment, but never with a view to injury and wrongdoing.' After World War II and the Nuremberg medical trials, it would be thought that the medical profession would maintain their independence from dictatorial regimes, put patients first and avoid falling into the trap again. Medical protocols—notably, the World Medical Association Declaration of Tokyo in 1975—prohibited medical complicity in torture.

Despite this, the involvement of doctors in state repression and abuse has, if anything, escalated since 1945. After World War II, state abuse, terrorism and torture continued to flourish, culminating in genocide as the century neared its close. Doctors have ruled a number of repressive regimes. Dictators from a medical background include Papa Doc Duvalier of Haiti, Hastings Banda of Malawi, Felix Houphouët-Boigny of the Ivory Coast and Bashar al-Assad of Syria. Various terrorist groups have also attracted medical leaders. Dr George Habash, leader of the Palestinian Front for the Liberation of Palestine was a paediatrician; Egyptian Dr Ayman al-Zawahiri, one of the world's most wanted terrorists,[2] is Osama bin Laden's personal physician and closest confidant.

Psychiatric abuses were routine in Eastern Europe, especially Russia. Enemies of the state were put in mental hospitals and subjected to extreme treatments to 'cure' them of dissident beliefs—in reality a form of punishment and torture. China and Cuba were involved in such practices as well.

The case of apartheid South Africa is illustrative of the role of doctors, psychiatrists and psychologists in planning and perpetuating human rights abuses. The architect of apartheid, Dr H.F. Verwoerd, trained in social psychology in Germany and America in the 1930s. Verwoerd was an extreme ideologue driving a policy of unparalleled social engineering. Although he portrayed apartheid as equitable to all races, he was indifferent to the appalling human consequences and disruption that will probably haunt the country for the foreseeable future. It will come as no surprise that the topic of Verwoerd's doctoral thesis was 'The blunting of affect'.

After the fall of apartheid, it was learned there had been medical abuse of suspects held by state security in prison for prolonged periods. Police surgeons had routinely sanctioned torture and violence towards prisoners, making no effort to provide medical care or intervene to protect their charges. The most notorious case was that of Black Power leader Steve Biko. Viciously beaten during interrogation by the Security Police, Biko was left naked in a coma on a cement floor, then transported in the back of a police van from Port Elizabeth to Pretoria. Before he died, he was examined by several police surgeons who claimed that he was faking or malingering symptoms.

There were numerous reports of doctors participating in the interrogation of captured insurgent soldiers in Namibia and Angola. The Aversion Project was run by psychiatrist Dr Aubrey Levin, who had the rank of colonel in the South African Defence Forces. It subjected not just homosexuals of both sexes, but those politically suspect and psychiatrically unwell. Over a protracted period from 1968 to 1987, there were extraordinary psychiatric practices with electric shock treatment and allegations of sex change operations for homosexual conscripts.

The most notorious medical offender in South Africa was the charmless Dr Wouter Basson (known like so many others as 'Doctor Death'). Basson started off as President P.W. Botha's cardiologist. In 1981, he joined the 7th SAMS Medical Battalion, heading a unit known as Project Coast, collecting information on chemical and biological warfare capabilities in other countries. Project Coast was involved in assassinations against the members of anti-apartheid movements. The ominously named Civil Cooperation Bureau hired Basson to supply lethal chemicals to use against popular black leaders in the anti-apartheid movement. Later he exported or sold ecstasy and Mandrax to drug dealers in communities active in the anti-apartheid movement.

Basson established a chemical and biological weapons program, investigating a project intended to put contraceptive agents into the water supply to the black population. The Namibian government sought his extradition over the death of South West Africa People's Organization (SWAPO) leaders thrown into the sea from a helicopter. In 1999, Basson faced 67 charges, including drug possession, drug trafficking, fraud and embezzlement of 36 million rand, 229 murders, conspiracy to murder and theft. After a 30-month trial, all charges were dismissed, raising dark murmurings of intervention in the judicial process. Other attempts to prosecute him failed, the Health Professionals Council was disinclined to investigate his activities and Basson remained in private practice as a cardiologist,[3] presumably on the basis that the only people he could now harm were apartheid supporters anyway.

Doctors have regularly been involved in state-sponsored torture. The doctor's role could extend from performing medical examinations before torture commenced—to show they were 'fit'—issuing false death certificates, ignoring injuries from torture when treating patients later, or participating in torture itself. Repressive regimes in the Middle East are regular offenders. There was wide publicity of the role of doctors who performed surgical amputation of the hands of thieves sentenced under Sharia law. Doctors have surgically removed ears as punishment for desertion in Saddam Hussein's Iraq. A doctor imprisoned at Abu Ghraib Prison in 1982 and 1983 reported there were over 1000 cases of prisoners killed by having blood taken from them for use in transfusions.

Doctors were frequently involved in repressive state practices in South America. In Uruguay, psychiatrists were involved in maintaining state repression in prisons. Dr Dolcey Britos was in charge of Libertad Prison, ensuring that suspect prisoners were abused and received the worst possible care. Following the Pinochet regime in Chile, at least nine army doctors were indicted for direct involvement in torture and injection of prisoners with pentothal during interrogation. In 1975 a School of Intelligence in Montevideo, Uruguay, ran 'practical courses in torture' in which participants took part in the torture of detainees brought there for that purpose. The detainees often lost consciousness but were revived by the course army doctor, Major Dr Roberto Scarabino Caravodosi.

During the Argentinean 'Dirty War' (1976–83), an estimated 400–500 babies were taken from young dissident parents, who then disappeared. Politically acceptable families, including military officers and police, then adopted the babies, although some families adopted the children in good faith. Doctors, including obstetricians, were involved in running this program.

Three secret centres had 'facilities' for pregnant women, including the Navy Mechanics School in Buenos Aires, also known as ESMA, and Naval intelligence headquarters at Mar del Plata, the regime's most notorious torture centre. Dr Norberto Bianco was in charge of the maternity ward at Campo de Mayo military hospital. Jailers gagged the women, forcing them to give birth blindfolded while tied to tables. Their babies were taken within minutes of delivery and adopted, often by the people who killed the mothers. Although some new mothers were led to believe they would be freed after the births, some were shot and others were thrown out of aircrafts over the Atlantic Ocean after being injected with sedatives by a navy doctor.

Stealing babies for rearing by 'acceptable' families was intended to create a new breed of 'super patriot', supportive of the army, who would lead Argentina into the twenty-first century. Operation Condor organised for some of the abducted children to be sent to Chile or Paraguay. Illegal adoptions for profit became a thriving business because the number of political prisoners was so high.

Just when it seemed as if nothing worse could occur, there was the Rwandan Genocide. Between April and May 1994, about 800,000 of 930,000 Tutsis were massacred by Hutus, including Hutu doctors and priests. At Butari Hospital, doctors refused to treat Tutsi patients or discharged them, well aware that death squads were waiting to receive them outside the hospital. At Kibcho Hospital, Dr Mutazihana directed the killings of patients in his hospital. Two senior members of the government that directed the genocide, physicians Dr Theodore Sindikubwabo and Dr Casimir Bizimungu, were later indicted for human rights abuses. Dr Clement Kayisherna, a governor, was sentenced to four life terms for inciting Hutus to kill Tutsis, including those who sought sanctuary in churches.

If one thing emerges from this study, it is that doctors, regardless of prestige, ability, qualification or training, are amongst the most willing accomplices of state abuse. They will play a leading role in perpetuating the system, support and participate in abuses and, where circumstances permit, willingly accede to the leadership of repressive regimes. There is no indication this is likely to change in future.

The basis for medical involvement in political abuse goes deep into the psychology of medicine and the personality of the practitioner. At its heart is an extreme grandiosity, a belief that 'treating' (in reality, extirpating) the illness affecting the nation is merely an extension of the ancient and honoured role of treating the sick patient.

This is summed up in the statement of Dr Mehmed Reşid before his suicide:

> Even though I am a physician, I cannot ignore my nationhood. Armenian traitors... were dangerous microbes. Isn't it the duty of a doctor to destroy these microbes? My Turkishness prevailed over my medical calling. Of course my conscience is bothering me, but I couldn't see my country disappearing. As to historical responsibility, I couldn't care less what historians of other nations write about me.

The attitude of the doctors who carried out the Armenian Genocide laid the template for the Holocaust. After the defeat in World War I, the Nazi government held out new promise and potential in the service of a vast national movement. For the Nazis, the therapeutic imperative was biological and the agents selected to carry this out were from the medical profession. The German medical profession was designated the central intellectual resource of the New Order.

Robert Lifton, the leading analyst of medical abuses in the Nazi concentration camps, regards the key feature of the medicalisation of killing as loss of the boundary between healing and killing. Medicalised killing required the use of vicious sadism, elaborate bureaucratic routine and the psychological motivation of the individuals involved. Killing occurred in two ways: by surgical means; that is, use of technology to avoid the effects of face-to-face involvement in killing; and what is referred to as 'killing as a therapeutic imperative'. The group being killed (Jews, gypsies, homosexuals, or earlier, the Armenians) was a threat to national identity and could be conceived of as a disease.

The central concept in Nazi ideology was the 'symbolisation of immortality'. Hitler's *Mein Kampf* was seething with such views, also expressed by Joseph Goebbels and Heinrich Himmler, among many others. As Rudolf Hess put it in 1934, 'National Socialism is nothing but applied biology.'

In this grotesquely thaumaturgic vision, the doctor was the final agent in the Nazi myth of therapy via mass murder. For the doctors at Auschwitz, killing was done in the name of healing. They could still rationalise that they were functioning as doctors, even pride themselves on making representations to save some individuals, and try to detach themselves at the same time. The means of doing so involved psychic numbing, diffusion of responsibility and derealisation, enhanced by heavy drinking. Only a 'sense of omnipotence' could protect the doctors from their own death anxiety in the concentration camp environment.

The final mechanism was 'doubling': the psychological creation of two separate selves. They spent the day as doctors supervising the process of exterminating other humans; then, they would go to their quarters and be a normal husband or father with their family.

While Mengele and Karadzic invariably attract attention, most doctors involved in political murder would be described as no more than time-servers, opportunistic careerists making the best of the situation and rationalising it in the name of a good cause. Yet behind each political killer, there is a profession. For each Auschwitz doctor performing barbaric experiments, there was an academician eagerly waiting to receive the skeletons, the pathological specimens and the test results. The South African medical profession paid no attention to complaints about police surgeons and it took Supreme Court action by a courageous group of doctors to get them to grudgingly commence proceedings against the Biko offenders.

If things later went wrong, they fell back on the morally tendentious 'Nuremberg defence': the routine response of morally atrophied nonentities.

15

The past, present and future of clinicide

We kill everybody, my dear. Some with bullets, some with words, and everybody with our deeds. We drive people into their graves, and neither see it nor feel it.

Maxim Gorky, *Enemies*

Clinicide does not occur in vacuum. It overlaps with murder by other health carers such as nurses, aides, technicians and physiotherapists. Just as the Shipman killings were being rationalised as a once-in-a-lifetime occurrence, it was learned that carer-assisted serial killing (CASK) was on the rise. CASK was described by toxicologist Dr Robert Forrest; the alternative term comes from Dr James Thunder, who refers to an epidemic of quiet killing.

The Virginia State Crime Commission investigating undetected elderly homicides in 2001 made the alarming claim that 65 per cent of all deaths of people over the age of 65 were not natural, occurring through active neglect, asphyxiation, starvation, under- or over-medication, suicide, poisoning, exposure, choking or arson. In 2003 in the United States, at least eighteen people were charged with killing a total of about 455 patients over 25 years. This did not take into account cases where killing was suspected but could not be proven, or there was not enough evidence to charge the suspects.

CASK is likely to escalate as the numbers of elderly patients in medical facilities and the medical personnel who have access to them increase. In the United States in 2000 there were over 33 million hospital admissions and 1.7 million residents of nursing homes; hospital employees numbered over 4 million and nursing home employees another 1.8 million. The year 2011 has special significance as this is when the baby-boomer generation reaches the age of 65 years.

This growing phenomenon, largely directed at elderly patients and children, is a reflection of the expanding institutionalisation of health care in a growing and aging population. The care of children and the elderly is taken away from the family home and put in the hands of 'service providers'. Caring for vulnerable charges in a place with easy access to potent drugs, there is significant potential for a murderous carer to cause havoc. Such crimes are difficult to detect and harder to prosecute. Many of the poisons (for example, a lethal dose of potassium chloride) are hard to detect within a short time of administration and, as was the case with many of Shipman's patients, the bodies may have been cremated.

Amongst the motives listed, in those who were charged, were acting out a sexual fantasy, demonstrating the need for a paediatric care unit in a rural hospital, impressing a boyfriend, exercising power over life and death, overcoming feelings of inadequacy and responding to requests for assisted suicide. Offenders included both medical and non-medical personnel—occasionally even hospital visitors. Typically the victims were all vulnerable: too sick, too old, too young to communicate or terminally ill. The extreme susceptibility of demented or frail patients with limited involvement of family members makes them ideal targets. In CASK, euthanasia is often cited as a defence by the killers.

Researchers Stark and Paterson found a minimum of thirteen health workers had murdered at least 170 patients between them in the past twenty years. Most of the cases involved nurses and many were women. Of 34 female serial murderers in the United States, six were nurses. The researchers believe it will be impossible to prevent people being employed who could go on to harm patients.

There were insufficient cases to build up a convincing psychological profile of the kind of care worker who could turn out to be a killer although some had a history of previous mental health problems. The best answer, they said, lies in being aware of the problem and responding as quickly as possible.

Death in the course of medical care is an accepted fact. A doctor specialising in palliative care (the care of terminally ill patients, frequently with cancer) would expect to have a 100 per cent mortality rate. The same mortality rate would be found in an institution caring for dementia patients. As the patients are in an advanced state of illness and often terminal, the CASK killer's defence is that (1) it cannot be shown that they did not die from natural causes, or (2) by administering lethal doses of morphine, muscle relaxants, electrolytes or suffocation, they were relieving suffering through euthanasia.

How were suspicions of foul play aroused? Some victims survived; perpetrators were seen alone with the patient or injecting medication that had not been ordered; syringes were left in a room; drugs had gone missing; rumours and gossip based on throwaway lines by offenders or awareness of their association with a high death rate. Once suspicions were raised, statistical auditing would soon reveal if something untoward was occurring when a suspect was on duty.

Many investigations were hampered by the period of time that had passed, cremation or deterioration of the bodies after burial, and the difficulty in detecting short-acting drugs after administration. One of the earliest documented cases occurred at the Archer Home for the Elderly and Infirm in Connecticut after World War I. There were 48 residents who died in the space of five years, an alarming statistic even given the higher rate of mortality expected among the 'elderly and infirm'. The last victim suddenly expired during the night of 30 May 1914 despite having appeared quite well previously. Post-mortem examinations established that very little of the prodigious quantity of arsenic purchased by the owner, Mrs Archer-Gilligan, to rid the home of rats was ever put to that use. In 1917, Mrs Archer-Gilligan was found guilty and sentenced to death, later certified insane and spent the rest of her days in an asylum, dying at the age of 59 in 1928.

Efren Saldivar (born 1969) murdered patients whilst working as a respiratory therapist at the Glendale Adventist Medical Center on the night shift. He killed patients by injecting drugs like morphine and Suxamethonium chloride which led to respiratory or cardiac arrest. The police exhumed the remains of patients who had died whilst Saldivar had been on duty. In March 2002 Saldivar pleaded guilty to six counts of murder and received six life sentences without parole. Statistical analysis indicates the total number of murders he committed could be as high as 120, but it will never be possible to confirm this due to the effects of decay of the bodies or cremation.

Nurse Donald Harvey is one of America's most prolific killers, murdering 36 patients over a fifteen-year period from the early 1970s to 1987 when he was finally caught. An amateur Satanist, he enjoyed spending time in the mortuary studying tissue samples and joked with the staff about 'getting rid of patients'. Facing trial, Harvey fell back on the euthanasia defence, claiming that what he did was 'mercy killing' despite the awful deaths he inflicted on patients with poison. Although convicted of 36 deaths, it is believed that he killed 87 people.

Critical care nurse Charles Cullen admitted to killing 30 to 40 patients during the sixteen years he worked as a nurse at ten hospitals in Pennsylvania and New Jersey. Cullen claimed he killed to alleviate the pain and suffering of his victims. Cullen made a plea bargain with prosecutors to avoid the death penalty by pleading guilty to 22 murders and attempted murder of six other cases.

One of the reasons why CASK and clinicide reach such levels in settings such as hospitals or nursing homes, is that deaths are expected to occur and attract little official attention. In recurring cases, the offenders do attract attention from colleagues, often receiving a morbid nickname. The Bailey case, if not many others, shows that the bureaucratic imperative is not one of enthusiastic investigation of suspicious cases. In Austria, 41 patients in a public hospital were murdered by four nurses in 1989. After the nurses were given long prison sentences, there was a marked increase in forensic autopsies in the succeeding years.

While it is tempting to include CASK with clinicide, there are good reasons for maintaining the distinction. An important difference between CASKs and clinicides is that the ultimate responsibility falls on the doctor, although care of the patient may be in the hands of many others. Doctors have a leading role in the culture of health care. The professional role of the doctor revolves around the oath-bound commitment to put the patient's interests first.

CASK and clinicide represent the ultimate perversion of medical care. It is an extreme paradox that as the medical profession has lost its independence and dominance of health care, CASKs can be expected to continue to increase with the growing role of other health carers to assume greater responsibility for patient care.

What measures can be taken to prevent clinicide? In general terms, these include:

- More vigilant checking of past employment, medical and criminal records when doctors are hired
- Compulsory reporting of all suspensions, firing or disciplining of doctors
- Any suspicious death in a hospital or nursing home needing to be treated as a crime scene, and staff being trained in how to do this
- Video camera surveillance, as used for the detection of hospital child abuse cases, being used to monitor suspect medical staff performing their duties
- Doctors being given better training in certifying death
- Where possible, autopsies, clinical or forensic, being required.

The most effective step, albeit least useful from the point of view of the victim, is the auditing of all deaths under medical care, including raising the percentage of autopsies done on routine deaths in hospitals, nursing homes and at home. The importance of this measure cannot be understated. The public should be educated that autopsy needs to be done more often in routine cases—and especially before cremation. This, like all forms of scrutiny and review, will need extra funding, especially for more qualified pathologists.

Indeed, as has been pointed out, there needs to be a massive education campaign of politicians and the public to understand that to have the least faulty (perfection being impossible to obtain) health care—the only reasonably certain hope of picking up medical murder early—there has to be an increase in costs that will dwarf anything contemplated at present.

It would have required very simple statistical methods to show that Shipman and Swango, in their respective settings, had an excessive patient death rate. The same would have applied to Bailey as psychiatric treatment should not lead to the 'piles of bodies' his practice produced. Intensive monitoring of deaths is even more important in quiet killing settings, and there is a burning imperative to ensure this becomes routine practice. Health care staff need training in the detection of the means of death in clinical situations. This is a woefully neglected area and without it all quality controls are likely to fail.

Prevention is as much a priority, going back to the selection of medical students. As soon as faculties elect to take students who are less narrowly focused and more aware of humanistic issues, complaints arise that they are too politically correct, or trying to produce doctors resembling social workers. Medical journals resonate with arguments for and against humanistic versus technologically adept doctors of the future. The answer to this is still to be determined.

Going back to the time of Osler, sagacious doctors say the same thing. The ideal doctor is not a scientific technician with a high IQ, but a pragmatic and dedicated practitioner with enough ability to both deal with the technical demands of a growing science and the emotional needs of a patient, rather than just the illness. Partly in response to this, partly in response to the crisis in confidence, has arisen an intense focus on research to demonstrate the qualities of professionalism, defined as an entity that requires the doctor to serve the interests of the patient above his or her self-interest. This aspires to altruism, accountability, excellence, duty, service, honour, integrity and respect for others.

Teaching students medical ethics is unfortunately, like many ideas, born of good intentions but hijacked by the agendas of the intellectuals who have to deliver the courses. This leads to the inevitable promotion of politically correct ideas like patient autonomy, the doctor as a service-provider and the need to be a political activist to change society for the better. The chances that force-feeding medical students, who tend to have a pragmatic attitude to their studies, with this propaganda will deter a potential killer is about nil and zero.

Psychopathic doctors cannot be trained to be sentient human beings but all doctors can be educated about the dangers of being compromised in the service of the state when working in prisons and the military. Medical ethics courses have tended to focus on the politically correct, but learning the history of the Armenian Genocide, the Nazi doctors and apartheid South Africa would have more benefit.

No one can be blamed for letting an unknown student who is a potential killer into medical training. Studies show that unprofessional behaviour at medical school is associated with later disciplinary action by medical boards. This manifests as irresponsibility or showing diminished ability to improve their behaviour, poor reliability, failing to complete clerking assignments, lack of initiative or motivation, poor relationships with other students or staff, or obvious anxiety or insecurity. Psychological screening and auditing of disciplinary problems throughout the medical course, if not residency, are required. Swango would have been detected very early in his training, and it is difficult to believe that Shipman would not have shown test findings that indicated a need for monitoring. Furthermore, regular testing would have the benefit of saving quite a few medical lives and careers likely to be lost through addiction, alcoholism and suicide.

Residency and speciality training are more critical times for assessment. There are far more opportunities for the lurking marauder to do as they wish with patients. Swango, of course, would not have progressed further, and it is likely that Shipman, already showing signs of drug dependence, would have come under scrutiny.

One area that is already showing results is the constant scrutiny of past legal or disciplinary offences. This will make it far harder to jurisdiction-hop but as Swango demonstrated, no system is perfect.

The problem of addicted doctors will always be a feature of medical practice. When Shipman was convicted, there was an outcry about his prior conviction some 24 years earlier for pethidine abuse. Yet at the time Shipman was examined by two psychiatrists, including a leading forensic specialist, there was no way they would have known that he was killing patients. The new approach adopted by medical boards of supervised programs for impaired physicians seems the most reasonable.

One issue that will not change is expecting medical colleagues to monitor their own kind with due vigilance. By definition, medicine is an autonomous activity often conducted in group settings. Most practitioners are acutely aware of the shortcomings of what they do. This results in a 'There but for the grace of God go I... ' mentality, an inner resistance to be overcome before reporting a colleague. As the story of Sir Roy Meadow's role in the false convictions of mothers accused of having Munchausen's syndrome by proxy indicates, overzealousness brings its own perils and the results are never good for medicine or society.

One issue that has not been discussed is what could be termed *system failure*. No doctor is ever trained in isolation of their colleagues, no doctor ever works apart from the society in which they practice. It cannot be too frequently stated that illness is a social construction, a reflection of the social and cultural values of a particular society at a particular time.

The problems in health care have spawned a burgeoning host of regulators, ranging from medical boards to health complaints units and the booming civil litigation system. The prosecuting business inevitably attracts a certain type of individual, often with an ideological, consumer-driven agenda, with the result in some legislatures being a new kind of medical Star Chamber. This adds to the burden of erring doctors, the majority of whom tend to be hapless minor offenders, while not doing much to prevent practitioners who are in essence criminal predators.

Clinicide will continue. It will always be discovered too late, although some of the more sensible measures may result in earlier intervention. Is there an answer to the patient who asks how they can know if the doctor to whom they entrust their care is a murderer?

Consider this statement, from the son of one of the Shipman's victims:

> I remember the time (Dr X) gave to my Dad. He would come over at the drop of a hat. He was a marvellous GP, apart from the fact that he killed my father.

After Shipman, there is no satisfactory answer to that question.

Acknowledgements

This book is dedicated to my late father Jeffery Kaplan, who I think would have approved (but wanted to know if dentists could be included).

Acknowledgements go to many people without whom this book could not have been written: my publishers Allen & Unwin; indefatigable agent and cooking collaborator Martin Kaplan; the ever-helpful librarians of Wollongong Hospital; Professor Colin Tatz for looking at the chapter on genocidal doctors; and Charles van Onselen, the Joe Silver of historians—for tolerance, support and encouragement above and beyond the call of duty, I cannot say enough.

Finally to Susan. Living with a madly deluded writer/historian/psychiatrist is a distinctly unusual business requiring special tolerance; this I was always granted without complaint.

Bibliography

For the preparation of this book, I have drawn on a wide range of sources on crime and criminology; history of medicine and society; forensic psychology, psychiatry and toxicology; medical cases and court reports; and biographies, news reports, and journal and magazine articles. Some of the more obscure or earlier killings were discovered in crime encyclopaedias, and other information could only be found in hard-to-obtain sources that are not in print.

To reproduce all the references would not only be unfriendly to the reader, but turn this book from a user-friendly edition into an academic tome. I have restricted the list as far as possible to acknowledge authorship and to list books and articles that illustrate important points or provide good accounts of a case.

I make special acknowledgement of several works that I have used extensively. Firstly, *Blind Eye: The terrifying story of a doctor who got away with murder* by James B. Steward is not only the main source of information on the life and crimes of Dr Michael Swango, but is a fine work of investigative journalism in a genre where sensationalism and over-statement are the norm. Steward played an important role in bringing the matter to the attention of the authorities, thereby ensuring that Swango was brought to justice before even more deaths occurred. This work should be a required text in journalism courses.

Secondly, Erik Larson's *The Devil in the White City: Murder, magic and madness at the fair that changed America*, a fictionalised account of the career of Herman Mudgett (aka H.H. Holmes) that shows how factual events can be presented in a flowing and gripping manner using novelistic techniques.

I thank both authors for their books, beg their indulgence for any omission of suitable credit, and highly recommend both works to readers.

With regard to general sources on medical history, the incomparable Roy Porter cannot be bettered, and it is difficult to believe that any future historian will provide us with a greater—and more succinct—account of the history of medicine in its social context than is found in *The Greatest Benefit to Mankind: A medical history of humanity from antiquity to the present.*

Two books that provide an excellent insight into forensic aspects of murder, as well as pointed comment on some cases I have reviewed, are Keith Simpson's *Forty Years of Murder* and John Emsley's *The Elements of Murder: A history of poison*, both of which include excellent accounts of other cases that will be of interest.

To ensure that readers understand that medical killers are only a very small number in the profession whose workers are trying to provide the highest level of medical care under difficult circumstances—albeit significantly different from those experienced by their predecessors—*Hippocratic Oaths: Medicine and its discontents* by Raymond Tallis is highly recommended.

Finally, while I have taken every effort to acknowledge sources, I apologise in advance for any omissions, misprints or inadvertent neglect; should these be discovered, I would be happy to include any corrections in subsequent editions—please contact the publishers.

General

A number of references, books and internet sites provided information on events, topics and people who are mentioned throughout the book.

These include the Wikipedia and TrueCrime websites, to which I am grateful for their ease of access, convenient layout and listing of other sources.

Camp, J. 1983, *One Hundred Years of Medical Murder*, Triad Panther Books, UnitedKingdom.

Emsley, J. 2005, *The Elements of Murder: A history of poison*, Oxford University Press.

Furneaux, R. 1957, *The Medical Murderer*, Abelard-Schuman, New York.

Gaute, J.H.H. & Odell, R. 1996, *The New Murderer's Who's Who*, Harrap Books, London.

Goodman, J. 1991, *The Medical Murders: Classic stories of true crime*, Warner Books, United Kingdom.

Hickey, E. 2003, *Encyclopedia of Murder and Violent Crime*, SAGE, United Kingdom.

——1996, *Serial Murderers and Their Victims*, Wadsworth Publishing Company, United Kingdom.

Irving, H.B. 2004, *A Book of Remarkable Criminals*, 1stWorld Library, 1stWorld Publishing.

Kaplan, R. 2007, 'The clinicide phenomenon: An exploration of medical murder', *Australasian Psychiatry*, August, 15(4):299–304.

Kinnell, H.G. 2000, 'Serial homicide by doctors: Shipman in perspective', *British Medical Journal*, December, 321(7276):1594–7.

Porter, R. 1997, *The Greatest Benefit to Mankind: A medical history of humanity from antiquity to the present*, HarperCollins, London.

Sifakis, C. 2001, *Encyclopedia of American Crime*, Facts On File, New York.

Simpson, K. 1980, *Forty Years of Murder*, Panther Books, United Kingdom.

Tallis, R. 2004, *Hippocratic Oaths: Medicine and its discontents*, Atlantic Books, United Kingdom.

Prologue

Cozanitis, D.A. 2004, 'One hundred years of barbiturates and their saint', *Journal of the Royal Society of Medicine*, December, 97(12):594–8.

Kaplan, R.M. 2006, 'The neuropsychiatry of shamanism', *Before Farming*, 2006/4, article 13.

Porter, R. 2003, *Quacks: Fakers and charlatans in English medicine*, NPI Media Group, United Kingdom.

Shim, J.K., Russ, A.J. & Kaufman, S.R. 2007, 'Clinical life: Expect-ation and the double edge of medical promise', *Health*, April, 11(2):245–64.

Smith, M. 1998, *Jesus the Magician: Charlatan or Son of God?* Ulysses Press, California.

2 Twentieth-century clinicide

Brower, M.C. & Price, B.H. 2001, 'Neuropsychiatry of frontal lobe dysfunction in violent and criminal behaviour: A critical review', *Journal of Neurology, Neurosurgery and Psychiatry*, December, 71(6):720–6.

Grombach, J. 1980, *The Great Liquidator*, Doubleday, New York.

Hardie, T.J. & Reed, A. 1998, 'Pseudologia fantastica, factitious disorder and impostership: A deception syndrome', *Medicine, Science and Law*, July, 38(3):198–201.

Hindler, C.G. 1989, 'Epilepsy and violence', *British Journal of Psychiatry*, August, 155 (2):246–9.

Iverson, K. 2002, *Demon Doctors: Physicians as serial killers*, Galen Press, Arizona.

Maeder, T. 1980, *The Unspeakable Crimes of Dr Petiot*, Little, Brown and Co., Boston.

Schlesinger, L.B. 2000, *Serial Offenders: Current thought, recent findings*, CRC Press, United States.

Seth, R. 1963, *Petiot: Victim of chance*, Hutchinson, London.

Weston, W.A. & Dalby J.T. 1991, 'A case of pseudologia fantastica with antisocial personality disorder', *Canadian Journal of Psychiatry*, October, 36(8):612–14.

3 Neurosurgeon with a needle

Katz, D. 2004, 'When Satan wears a stethoscope', *The American Journal of Bioethics*, Winter, 4(1):63–4.

LaDuca, T., 'Competence and the Laying of Blame', *Medical Education*, 35(12):1170–1171.

LeDuff, C. 2000, 'Man to admit to murdering 3 L.I. patients', *New York Times*, 6 September.

McCarthy, M. 2000, 'US doctor pleads guilty to murdering patients', *Lancet*, September, 356(9234):1010.

Quirey, Jr, Esquire, William O. & Adams, J., Esquire, 'National Practitioner Data Bank revisited: the lessons of Michael Swango, M.D.', *Viriginia State Bar* http://www.vsb.org/sections/hl/bank.pdf.

Scheck, A. 2001, 'Using sensitive forensic testing: Lab cracks the Dr. Death case', *Emergency Medicine News*, February, 23(2):51–2.

Segel, L. 2003, 'Licence to kill', *Medical Post*, May, 39(19):44.

Steward, James B. 1999, *Blind Eye: The terrifying story of a doctor who got away with murder*, Touchstone, New York.

Taylor, G.J. 2005, 'Physician as serial killer', *New England Journal of Medicine*, July, 353(4):430.

Waters, T.M. et al. 2006, 'The role of the National Practitioner Data Bank in the credentialing process', *American Journal of Medical Quality*, January/February 21(1):30–9.

Woods, D. 2000, 'US doctor may have killed 60', *British Medical Journal*, September, 321(7262):657.

20/20 Interview with Michael Swango by John Stossel, aired 13 February 1986.

20/20 Special Report on Michael Swango, aired 18 August 1999.

ABC News transcript, interview with author James B. Stewart, author of *Blind Eye*, aired 19 August 1999.

http://www.africaresource.com/index.php?option=com_content&view=article&id=367:africa-and-western-medical-malpractices&catid=117:science&Itemid=361

http://www.cbsnews.com/stories/2000/07/12/national/main214413.shtml

http://www.columbusoh.about.com/library/weekly/aa090600a.htm

http://www.edition.cnn.com/2000/LAW/07/18/doctor.killings/

http://www.enquirer.com/editions/2000/10/19/loc_former_doctor_says.html

http://www.gcn.com/print/vol20_no15/4458–1.html?topic=news

http://www.highbeam.com/doc/1G1–66168860.html

http://www.newyorker.com/archive/1997/11/24/1997_11_24_090_TNY_CARDS_000381235

http://www.parkridgecenter.org/Page148.html

http://www.politedissent.com/archives/1312

http://www.vamalpractice.info/Adobe%20pdf/Swango/Swango%20Indictment.pdf

4 Doctor as demiurge

Arnetz, B.B. et al. 1987, 'Suicide patterns among physicians related to other academics as well as to the general population: Results from a national long-term prospective study and a retrospective study', *Acta Psychiatrica Scandinavica*, February, 75(2):139–43.

Balint, M. 1955, 'The doctor, his patient, and the illness', *Lancet*, April, 268(6866):683–8.

Barsky, A.J. 1988, 'The paradox of health', *New England Journal of Medicine*, 18 February, 318(7):414–18.

Beeson, P.B. 1986, 'One hundred years of American internal medicine: A view from the inside', *Annals of Internal Medicine*, September, 105(3):436–44.

Coury, C. 1967, 'The basic principles of medicine in the primitive mind', *Medical History*, April, 11(2):111–27.

Dalrymple-Champneys, W. 1955, 'The medical student through the ages', *Proceedings of the Royal Society of Medicine*, October, 48(10):789–98.

Fitzgerald, F.T. 1994, 'The tyranny of health', *New England Journal of Medicine*, July, 331(3):196–8.

Gabassi, P.G. et al. 2002, 'Burnout syndrome in the helping professions', *Psychology Reports*, February, 90(1):309–14.

Grant, W.B. 1980, 'The hated patient and his hating attendants', *Medical Journal of Australia*, December, 2(13):727–9.

Hale, H. 1973, 'How our patients make us ill', *Advances in Psychiatric Treatment*, May, 3(5):254.

Harmer, M. 2005, 'Shipman and the anaesthetist', *Anaesthesia*, February, 60(2):111–12.

Hodges, B., Regehr, G. & Martin, D. 2001, 'Difficulties in recognizing one's own incompetence: Novice physicians who are unskilled and unaware of it', *Academic Medicine*, October, 76(10):S87–9.

Jackson, S.W. 2001, 'The wounded healer', *Bulletin of the History of Medicine*, Spring, 75(1):1–36.

Johnson, W.D. 1991, 'Predisposition to emotional distress and psychiatric illness amongst doctors: The role of unconscious and experiential factors', *British Journal of Medical Psychology*, December, 64(Pt 4):317–29.

Prodgers, A. 1999, 'On hating the patient', *British Journal of Psychotherapy*, 8(2):144–154.

Shanahan, F., Quigley, F. & Eamonn, M.M. 2006, 'Medicine in the Age of "Ulysses": James Joyce's portrait of life, medicine, and disease on a Dublin day a century ago', *Perspectives in Biology and Medicine*, Spring, 49(2):276–85.

Shorter, E. 1997, *A History of Psychiatry: From the era of the asylum to the age of Prozac*. John Wiley & Sons, New York City.

Stern, D.T. & Papadakis, M. 2006, 'The developing physician: Becoming a professional', *New England Journal of Medicine*, October, 355(17):1794–9.

5 Early medical murder

Davenport-Hines, R. 2004, 'Palmer, William [the Rugeley Poisoner] (1824–1856)', *Oxford Dictionary of National Biography*, Oxford University Press.

Goodman, J. (ed.) 1990, *Medical Murders*, Piatkus, London.

Knott, G.H. 1912, *The Trial of William Palmer*, William Hodge & Co., Edinburgh.

Larson, E. 2003, *The Devil in the White City: Murder, magic and madness at the fair that changed America*, Transworld Publishers, London.

McLaren, A. 1995, *A Prescription for Murder: The Victorian serial killings of Dr. Thomas Neill Cream*, University of Chicago Press.

O'Neill, B. 1986, 'The last public execution in Glasgow: The case of Dr Edward Pritchard, M.D.', *Scottish Medical Journal*, October, 31(4):256–60.

http://www.public-domain-content.com/books/Criminals/C5P1.shtml

http://www.williampalmer.co.uk/

6 A doctor's own story

Clarkson, W. 2005, *Evil Beyond Belief: How and why Dr Harold Shipman murdered more than 300 people*, John Blake.

Dyer, C. 1998, 'British GP may face further murder charges', *British Medical Journal*, October, 317(17):1033.

Esmail, A. 2005, 'Physician as serial killer: The Shipman case', *New England Journal of Medicine*, May, 352(18):1843–4.

Henriques, J. 2003, 'The role of forensic science in the trial of Harold Shipman', *Medicine, Science and the Law*, 43(33):185–8.

Kaplan, R. 2001, 'Murder by medical malice: The love–hate relationship between Dr Harold Shipman and his patients', *South African Medical Journal*, June, 91(6):492.

O'Neill, B. 2000, 'Doctor as murderer: Death certification needs tightening up, but it still might not have stopped Shipman', *British Medical Journal*, February, 320(7231):329–30.

Sitpond, M. 2000, *Addicted to Murder: The true story of Dr Harold Shipman*, Virgin, London.

Soothill, K. 2001, 'The Harold Shipman case: A sociological perspective', *Journal of Forensic Psychiatry and Psychology*, September, 12(2):260–2.

Soothill, K. & Wilson, D. 2005, 'Theorising the puzzle that is Harold Shipman', *Journal of Forensic Psychiatry & Psychology*, December, 16(4):685–98.

Warf, B. & Waddell, C. 2002, 'Heinous spaces, perfidious places: The sinister landscapes of serial killers', *Social & Cultural Geography*, September, 3(3):323–45.

Whittle, B. & Ritchie, J. 2000, *Harold Shipman: Prescription for murder*, Time Warner Paperbacks, London.

7 Searching for Shipman

Ashraf, H. 2002, 'At least 215 people killed by UK doctor, says official inquiry', *Lancet*, July, 360(9329):317.

Baker, R. 2004, 'Patient-centred care after Shipman', *Journal of the Royal Society of Medicine*, April, 97(4):161–5.

Horton, R. 2001, 'The real lessons from Harold Frederick Shipman', *Lancet*, January, 357(9250):82–3.

Kaplan, R. 2006, 'Harold Shipman: An awful sod', *Australasian Psychiatry*, March, 14(1):90–3.

Peters, C. 2005, *Harold Shipman: Mind set on murder*, Carlton Books, Great Britain.

Pollard, J.S. 2003, 'The Shipman case and its legacy', *Medico-Legal Journal*, 71(Pt 2):47–60.

Pounder, D.J. 2003, 'The case of Dr. Shipman', *American Journal of Forensic Medicine and Pathology*, September, 24(3):219–26.

Ramsay, S. 2001, 'Audit further exposes UK's worst serial killer', *Lancet*, January, 357(9250):123–4.

Schlesinger, L.B. 2007, 'Sexual homicide: Differentiating catathymic and compulsive murders', *Aggression and Violent Behavior*, March–April, 12(2) 2007:242–56.

Smith, D.J. 2005, 'The Shipman Inquiry: Independent Public Inquiry into the issues arising from the case of Harold Fredrick Shipman'. *The Shipman Inquiry* http://www.the-shipman-inquiry.org.uk/

Van Weel, C. 2004, 'Clinicians' autonomy till the bitter end: Can we learn from the extraordinary case of Harold Shipman?', *Netherlands Journal of Medicine*, July–August, 62(7):261–3.

8 More medical murder

Cullen, L. 1998, 'Some reflections on the case of Dr. Pritchard', *Proceedings of the Royal College of Physicians of Edinburgh*, April, 28(2):187–97.

Cullen, P.V. 2006, *A Stranger in Blood: The case files on Dr John Bodkin Adams*, Elliott & Thompson, London.

Davis, V. 2004, 'Murder, we wrote', *British Journalism Review*, 15(1):56–62.

Devlin, P. 1985, *Easing the passing: The trial of Doctor John Bodkin Adams*, The Bodley Head, London.

Farber, M. 1982, *'Somebody Is Lying': The story of Dr. X*, Doubleday, New York.

Gow, J.G. 1987, 'Easing the passing: The trial of Dr John Bodkin Adams', *Journal of the Royal Society of Medicine*, July, 80(7):470.

Hallworth, R. & Williams, M. 1983, *Where There's a Will . . . The sensational life of Dr John Bodkin Adams*, Capstan Press, Jersey.

Hoskins, P. 1984, *Two Men Were Acquitted: The trial and acquittal of Doctor John Bodkin Adams*, Secker and Warburg, London.

Huxtable, R. 2004, 'Get out of jail free? The doctrine of double effect in English law', *Palliative Medicine*, 18(1):62–8.

Robson, H.E. 1983, 'Dr. John Bodkin Adams', *British Journal of Sports Medicine*, September, 17(3):183.

Simon, M.A. 1985, *Science and Justice: The case of Dr. Jascalevich*, SAGE, United Kingdom.

Simpson, K. 1971, 'Medicine v. the Law: part heard', *Australian Journal of Forensic Sciences*, March, 3(3): 114–120.

Surtees, J. 2000, *The Strange Case of Dr. Bodkin Adams: The life and murder trial of Eastbourne's infamous doctor and the views of those who knew him*, SB Publications, United Kingdom.

Thomas, B. 2002, *Law and Literature*, Gunter Narr Verlag.

'Acquittal of Dr. J. Bodkin Adams: Judge's summing-up', *British Medical Journal*, April 1957, 1(5024):954–5.

'Dr. Jascalevich settles a malpractice lawsuit', *New York Times*, 3 December 1981.

http://www.everything2.com/node/1930290

http://laurajames.typepad.com/clews/2005/07/the_murder_case.html

http://www.shyscyberchamber.com/adams_bodkin.asp

http://www.strangerinblood.co.uk/html/case.htm

New York Times Co. v. Jascalevich, 439 U.S. 1317 (1978). U.S. Supreme Court.

'Serial killers "attracted to medical profession"', *Independent*, 10 May 2001.

'Suspect spend 4 years at Riverdell: Has New York license resigned in 1967', *New York Times*, 17 March 1976.

'Trial of Dr. J. Bodkin Adams: Expert evidence', *British Medical Journal*, April 1957, 1(5022):828–34.

'Trial of Dr. J. Bodkin Adams: Expert evidence continued', *British Medical Journal*, April 1957, 1(5023):889–94.

9 Murdering the madam

Anspacher, C. 1965, *The Trial of Dr. De Kaplany*, Frederick Hill, Inc., New York.

Cohen, D. 2001, 'University lecturer accused of murdering his wife', *Guardian*, 1 May.

Coley, N.G. 1991, 'Alfred Swaine Taylor, MD, (1806–1880): Forensic toxicologist', *Medical History*, October, 35(4):409–27.

L'etang, H. 1974, 'Drinking and politicking', *Alcohol and Alcoholism*, 9(2):70–2.

McLaren, A. 1995, *A Prescription for Murder: The Victorian serial killings of Dr. Thomas Neill Cream*, University of Chicago Press.

Marks, V. & Richmond, C. 2008, 'Colin Bouwer: Professor of psychiatry and murderer', *Journal of the Royal Society of Medicine*, August, 101(8):400–8.

Rosenfeld, L. 1985, 'Alfred Swaine Taylor (1806–1880), pioneer toxicologist—and a slight case of murder', *Clinical Chemistry*, July, 31(7):1235–6.

Watson, K.D. 2006, 'Medical and chemical expertise in English trials for criminal poisoning, 1750–1914', *Medical History*, July, 50(3): 373–90.

'Bouwer loses murder appeal', *Press*, 25 June 2002.

Murder Casebook, *Deadly Doctors: Carl Coppolino and Geza De Kaplany*, Marshall Cavendish, United Kingdom, 1991.

10 Surgeons, sick and sinister

Cherian, S.M., Nicks, R. & Lord, R.S. 2001, 'Ernst Ferdinand Sauerbruch: Rise and fall of the pioneer of thoracic surgery', *World Journal of Surgery*, August, 25(8):1012–20.

Dewey M., Schagen U., Eckart W.U. & Schönenberger E. 2006, 'Ernst Ferdinand Sauerbruch and his ambiguous role in the period of National Socialism', *Annals of Surgery*, August, 244(2):315–21.

Dunbar, J.A. et al. 2007, 'In the wake of hospital inquiries: Impact on staff and safety', *Medical Journal of Australia*, January, 186(2):80–3.

Ernst, E. 2001, 'Commentary: The Third Reich—German physicians between resistance and participation', *Intern-ational Journal of Epidemiology*, 30:37–42.

Groves, J.E., Dunderdale, B.A. & Stern, T.A. 2002, 'Celebrity patients, VIPs, and potentates', *Primary Care Companion to the Journal of Clinical Psychiatry*, December, 4(6):215–223.

Marston, A. 1999, *Hamilton Bailey: A surgeon's life*, Greenwich Medical Media, London.

Paton, A. 1999, 'Hamilton Bailey: A surgeon's life', *British Medical Journal*, July, 319(7204):265.

Youngson, R.M. 1997, 'The demented surgeon is operating' in R.M. Youngson, *Medical Curiosities*, Carroll & Graf, New York.

http://www.time.com/time/magazine/article/0,9171,855835,00.html

11 The deepest sleep

Bromberger, B. & Fife-Yeomans, J. 1991, *Deep Sleep: Harry Bailey and the scandal of Chelmsford*, Simon & Schuster, Australia.

Ellard, J. 1991, 'Chelmsford and its aftermath', *Psychiatric Bulletin*, 15(11):686–8.

John, D. 1993, 'Deep sleep: Australian doctors escape discipline', *British Medical Journal*, June, 306(6891):1501.

Lupton, D. 1993, 'Back to bedlam? Chelmsford and the press', *Australian and New Zealand Journal of Psychiatry*, March, 27(1):140–8.

Slattery, J.P. The Honourable Acting Justice 1990, Report of the Royal Commission into Deep Sleep Therapy, The Commission, Sydney.

Stolk, P.J. 1968, 'Adolf Hitler: His life and his illness', *Psychiatria, Neurologia, Neurochirurgia*, September–October, 71(5):381–98.

Swan, N. 1991, 'Australian deep sleep report awakens anger', *British Medical Journal*, January, 302(6768):70–1.

12 Killing with kindness

Bamgbose, O. 2004, 'Euthanasia: Another face of murder', *International Journal of Offender Therapy and Comparative Criminology*, February, 48(1):111–21.

Barkham, P. 2000, 'Doctors of death', *Guardian*, 27 January.

Belluck, P. 1999, 'Dr. Kevorkian is a murderer, the jury finds', *New York Times*, 22 March.

Cohen, L. et al. 2005, 'Accusations of murder and euthanasia in end-of-life care', *Journal of Palliative Medicine*, December, 8(6):1096–1104.

Cook, G.C. 2006, 'The practice of euthanasia at the highest level of society: The Lords Dawson (1864–1945) and Horder (1871–1955)', *Journal of Medical Biography*, May, 14(2):90–2.

Devlin, P. 1985, *Easing the Passing: The trial of Dr John Bodkin Adams*, The Bodely Head, London.

Fergusson, A. 1996, 'Editorial's objectivity is in doubt', *British Medical Journal*, July, 313(7051):228a–22.

Kottow, M.H. 1988, 'Euthanasia after the Holocaust: Is it possible?—a report from the Federal Republic of Germany', *Bioethics*, January, 2(1):58–9.

Marker, R. & Hamlon, K. 1999, 'Prisoner number 284797', *Human Life Review*, Summer, 25(3):65–76.

Quill, T.E. 1991, 'Death and dignity: A case of individualized decision making', *New England Journal of Medicine*, March, 324:691–4.

Ramsay, J.H. 1994, 'A king, a doctor, and a convenient death', *British Medical Journal*, May, 308(6941):1445.

Roberts, J. & Kjellstrand, C. 1996, 'Jack Kevorkian: A medical hero', *British Medical Journal*, June, 312(7044):1434.

Simpson, W.G. 1997, 'A different kind of Holocaust: From euthan-asia to tyranny', *Linacre Quarterly*, August, 64(3):87–92.

Smith, W.J. 1998, 'The Serial Killer as Folk Hero: Kevorkian proceeds with his plan', *Weekly Standard*, 7 June 1998, vol.3, no.42.

Strous, R.D. 1957, 'Trial of Dr. J. Bodkin Adams: Expert evidence', *British Medical Journal*, April, 1(5022):828–34.

Surtees, J. 2000, *The Strange Case of Dr. Bodkin Adams: The life and murder trial of Eastbourne's infamous doctor and the views of those who knew him*, Lewes, United Kingdom.

Zinn, C. 2001, 'Doctor sets up "how to die" workshops in New Zealand', *British Medical Journal*, February, 322:315.

'Acquittal of Dr. J. Bodkin Adams: Judge's summing-up', *British Medical Journal*, April 1957, 1(5024):954–5.

Americas Profile: Dr Death. http://news.bbc.co.uk/2/hi/americas/222218.stm

Euthanasia Special Report, '"Dr Death": Pushing the law', 28 November 2000. http://news.bbc.co.uk/2/hi/health/back-ground_briefings/euthanasia/331269.stm

Euthanasia Special Report, 'Lessons from Down Under'. 28 November 2000. http://news.bbc.co.uk/2/hi/health/background_briefings/euthanasia/331271.stm

'Frail and smiling, "Dr. Death" walks out of prison', 1 June 2007. http://www.cnn.com/2007/LAW/06/01/kevorkian.release.ap/index.html

'The King's Peace? The death of King George V', *Times*, 28 November 1986.

13 Psychiatrist of the Bosnian Genocide

Cigar, N. 1995, *Genocide in Bosnia: The policy of ethnic cleansing*, Texas A&M University Press.

Danner, M. 1998, 'Bosnia: The turning point', *New York Review of Books*, 5 February, pp. 34–41.

——1998, 'Bosnia: The great betrayal', *New York Review of Books*, 26 March, pp. 40–52.

Dekleva, K.B. & Post, J.M. 1997, 'Genocide in Bosnia: The case of Dr. Radovan Karadzic', *Journal of the American Academy of Psychiatry and the Law*, 25(4):485–96.

Guinan, M.E. 1993, 'War crimes of the 90s: Rape as a strategy', *Journal of the American Medical Women's Association*, March–April, 48(2):59, 61.

Jerrold, M. & Post, A.G. 2004, *Leaders and Their Followers in a Dangerous World: The psychology of political behavior*. Cornell University Press.

Kaplan, R.M. 2003, 'Dr Radovan Karadzic: Psychiatrist, poet, soccer coach and genocidal leader', *Australasian Psychiatry*, March 11(1):74–8.

Redlich, F. 2000, *Hitler: Diagnosis of a psychopathic prophet*, Oxford University Press, New York.

Robins, R. 1986, 'Paranoid ideation and charismatic leadership', *Psychohistory Review*, 6:15–55.

Weine, S.M. 1999, *When History Is a Nightmare: Lives and memories of ethnic cleansing in Bosnia-Herzogevina*, Rutgers University Press, London.

Weine, S.M. et al. 1995, 'Psychiatric consequences of "ethnic cleansing": Clinical assessments and trauma testimonies of newly resettled Bosnian refugees', *American Journal of Psyc-hiatry*,152:536–42.

American Psychiatric Association 1998, 'The principles of medical ethics with annotations especially applicable to psychiatry', American Psychiatric Association, Washington DC.

14 Genocidal doctors

Ascherson, N. 1987, 'The Death Doctors', *New York Review of Books*, May, vol.34, no.9.

Baron, J.H. 1999, 'Genocidal doctors', *Journal of the Royal Society of Medicine*, November, 92(11):590–3.

Charatan, F. 1999, 'Brazil challenges doctors accused of torture', *British Medical Journal*, March, 318(7186):757.

Cilasun, U. 1991, 'Torture and the participation of doctors', *Journal of Medical Ethics*, 17:s21–2.

Cohen, J.H. & Cohen, E.L. 1958, 'Doctor Marat and his skin', *Journal of Medical History*, October, 2(4):281–6.

Curran, W.J. 1979, 'Law–medicine notes: The Guyana mass suicides—medicolegal re-evaluation', *New England Journal of Medicine*, June, 300(23):1321.

Dadrian, V.N. 1986, 'The role of Turkish physicians in the World War I genocide of Ottoman Armenians', *Holocaust and Genocide Studies*, 1(2):169–192.

——1997, 'The Turkish Military Tribunal's Prosecution of the Authors of the American Genocide: Four major court-martial series', *Holocaust and Genocide Studies*, 11(1):28–59.

——2004, 'Patterns of twentieth-century genocides: The Armenian, Jewish, and Rwandan cases', *Journal of Genocide Research*, 6(4):487–522.

Davison, P. 1998, 'Ex-Argentine leader on baby-snatching charges', *Independent* (London), 10 July 1998.

Eckert, W.G. 1982, 'Physician crimes and criminals: The histo-rical and forensic aspects', *American Journal of Forensic Medicine and Pathology*, September, 3(3):221–30.

Gurvich, M., 'Baby-snatching: Argentine dirty war secret'. http://www.consortiumnews.com/archive/story44.html

Hanauske-Abel, H.M. 1996, 'Not a slippery slope or sudden subversion: German medicine and national socialism in 1933', *British Medical Journal*, 313(7070):1453–63.

Harris, S.H. 1994, *Factories of Death: Japanese biological warfare—1932–45 and the American cover-up*, Routledge, New York.

Jenkins, T. & McLean, G.R. 2004, 'The Steve Biko affair', *Lancet*, December, 364, Supplement 1:s36–7.

Justo, L. 2006, 'Doctors, interrogation, and torture', *British Medical Journal*, June, 332(7556):1462–3.

Kaplan, R.M. 2004, 'Treating homosexuality as a sickness: Psychiatric abuses during apartheid era have not been brought to account', *British Medical Journal*, April, 328(7445):956.

Kater, M.H. 1987, 'Hitler's early doctors: Nazi physicians in predepression Germany', *Journal of Modern History*, March, 59(1):25–52

Lifton, R.J. 1982, 'Medicalized killing in Auschwitz', *Psychiatry*, November, 45(4):283–97.

—— 1986, *The Nazi Doctors: Medical killing and the psychology of genocide*, Basic Books, New York.

——2004, 'Doctors and torture', *New England Journal of Medicine*, July, 351(5):415–16.

Lucas, T. & Pross, C. 1995, 'Caught between conscience and complicity: Human rights violations and the health professions', *Medical and Global Survival*, June, 2(2):106–14.

Nightingale, E.O. 1990, 'The role of physicians in human rights', *Law, Medicine and Health Care*, Spring–Summer, 18(1–2):132–9.

Peiffer, J. 2006, 'Phases in the postwar German reception of the "Euthanasia Program" (1939–1945) involving the killing of the mentally disabled and its exploitation by neuroscientists', *Journal of the History of the Neurosciences*, September, 15(3):210–44.

Riding, A. 1987, 'Argentines fight for orphans of a dirty war', *New York Times*, 30 December.

Seeman, M.V. 2005, 'Psychiatry in the Nazi era', *Canadian Journal of Psychiatry*, March, 50(4):218–25.

Seidelman, W.E. 1988, 'Mengele medicus: Medicine's Nazi heritage', *The Milbank Quarterly*, 66(2):221–39.

Simpson, W.G. 2006, 'Hitler's psychiatrists: Healers and researchers turned executioners and its relevance today', *Harvard Review of Psychiatry*, January–February, 14(1):30–7.

Strous, R.D. 2006, 'Nazi euthanasia of the mentally ill at Hadamar', *American Journal of Psychiatry*, January, 163(1):27.

Suedfeld, P. 1990, 'Psychologists as victims, administrators and designers of torture', in Suedfeld, P. (ed.), *Psychology and Torture*, Hemisphere Publishing, New York, pp. 101–114.

Wenzel, T. 2007, 'Torture', *Current Opinion in Psychiatry*, September, 20(5):491–6.

Wessely, S. 2007, 'When doctors become terrorists', *New England Journal of Medicine*, August, 357(7):635–7.

Williams, P. 1989, *Unit 731: Japan's secret biological warfare in World War II*, Free Press, United States.

Amnesty International 1994, Amnesty International Annual Report, London.

British Medical Association 1992, *Medicine betrayed: The participation of doctors in human rights abuses—Report of a working party*, Zed Books, London.

15 The past, present and future of clinicide

Brainard, A.H. & Brislen, H.C. 2007, 'Viewpoint: Learning professionalism—a view from the trenches', *Academic Medicine*, November, 82(11):1010–14.

Burton, J.L. & Underwood, J. 2007, 'Clinical, educational, and epidemiological value of autopsy', *Lancet*, April, 369(9571):1471–80.

Calman, K. 1994, 'The profession of medicine', *British Medical Journal*, October, 309(6962):1140–3.

Coats, A.J. 2001, 'Medical malpractice, murder and the academic community: Trouble ahead', *International Journal of Cardi-ology*, June, 79(1):1–4.

Cohen, J.J. 2007, 'Viewpoint: Linking professionalism to humanism—what it means, why it matters', *Academic Medicine*, November, 82(11):1029–32.

Crow, S.M. et al. 2003, 'A prescription for the rogue doctor: part I—begin with diagnosis', *Clinical Orthopaedics and Related Research*, June, (411):334–9.

——2003, 'A prescription for the rogue doctor: Part II—ready, aim, fire', *Clinical Orthopaedics and Related Research*, June, (411):340–5.

Hale, R. 1992, 'The cobbler's children: How the medical profession looks after its own', *British Journal of Hospital Medicine*, March, 47(6):405, 407.

Kessler, D.P., Summerton, N. & Graham, J.R. 2006, 'Effects of the medical liability system in Australia, the UK, and the USA', *Lancet*, July, 368(9531):240–6.

Kuczewski, M.G. 2007, 'The soul of medicine', *Perspectives in Biology and Medicine*, Summer, 50(3):410–20.

Rucinski, J. & Cybulska, E. 1985, 'Mentally ill doctors', *British Journal of Hospital Medicine*, February, 33(2):90–4.

Silove, D. 1995, 'The psychiatrist as a political leader in war: Does the profession have a monitoring role?', *Journal of Nervous and Mental Disease*, 183:125–6, 1995.

Stark, C. et al. 1997, 'Nurses who kill: Serial murder in healthcare institutions', *Nursing Times*, vol.93, no.3–7.

Stark, C., Paterson, B. & Kidd, B. 2001, 'Opportunity may be more important than profession in serial homicide', *British Medical Journal*, April, 322:993–993.

Thunder, J.M. 2003, 'Quiet killings in medical facilities: Detection and prevention', *Issues in Law and Medicine*, Spring, 18(3):211–37.

Yorker, B.C. et al. 2006, 'Serial murder by healthcare professionals', *Journal of Forensic Science*, November, 51(6):1362–71.

Endnotes

Chapter 1
1. Nesset is usually listed as a doctor but two accounts state that he was a medical administrator.

Chapter 3
1. Necrophilia: obsession, to the point of sexual compulsion, with death.
2. The name Swango is of Welsh origin.

Chapter 4
1. When justice caught up with him, Burke was hanged and dissected; a purse made from his skin is displayed at the Edinburgh Police Museum.

Chapter 5
1. As an interesting aside, Joseph Lis (aka Joe Silver), the character identified as Jack the Ripper by Charles van Onselen in his book *The Fox and the Flies*, started off as a feltscher, a barber who did small surgical procedures.
2. Showing that life and art are seldom far apart, the Ripper murders coincided with two significant literary events: the theatrical launching of Robert Louis Stevenson's *Dr Jekyll and Mr Hyde*, and the publishing debut of the greatest detective in literary history, Sherlock Holmes, in *The Study in Scarlet* by Conan Doyle.

Chapter 6

1. No one seems to have ever confirmed the exact spelling of Shipman's middle name; 'Frederick' is the common version used.
2. Sloane's Liniment is a preparation rubbed on the skin for muscle pain that Shipman used during his rugby days.

Chapter 7

1. Robert Brittain was a Scottish forensic pathologist who wrote a classic paper on sadistic serial killers; see Bibliography.

Chapter 8

1. While Nesset is usually listed as a medical doctor, details of his medical background and training are not available to the non-Norwegian reader.

Chapter 10

1. Always known as Hamilton Bailey.

Chapter 11

1. There has been an attempt to explain Adolf Hitler's behaviour on this basis.

Chapter 12

1. Carer-assisted serial killing, see Chapter 15.
2. The role of the doctors who administered the program will be discussed in greater detail in Chapter 14.
3. At the time of writing, January 2008.

Chapter 14

1. One of the few doctors to make a full commitment to resisting the Nazis was George Groscurth, at one time one of Joseph Goebbels's doctors. He helped Jewish doctors and leaked information to the Resistance before he was hanged in 1944.
2. Now reported to have been killed.
3. At the time of writing, it is reported that there are attempts to remove Basson from the register.